THE MEANING OF THE
WORLD IS LOVE

RICHARD CLEMENTS

The Meaning of the World Is Love

Selected Texts from
Hans Urs von Balthasar
with Commentary

IGNATIUS PRESS   SAN FRANCISCO

Cover art:
Casey Horner/Unsplash.com

Cover design by Enrique J. Aguilar

ISBN 978-1-62164-351-7 (PB)
ISBN 978-1-64229-210-7 (eBook)
Library of Congress Control Number 2021941886
Printed in the United States of America ∞

For my wife, Jessica,
and for our children: Madeline, Peter,
John, Marissa, and Sophia

ACKNOWLEDGMENTS

The writings of Hans Urs von Balthasar have significantly influenced not only the writing of this book, but also my own understanding of what life and love are all about. I am deeply indebted to him.

Many thanks go to the editors at Ignatius Press for their insightful comments and suggestions regarding the manuscript for this book. Many thanks also go to my wife, Jessica, and to our children, Madeline, Peter, John, Marissa, and Sophia, for their love and support throughout the writing of this book.

CONTENTS

INTRODUCTION:
A THEOLOGY OF LOVE

Why in fact *is* there something rather than
nothing? The question remains open regardless
of whether one affirms or denies the existence of
an absolute being [God]. If there is no absolute
being, what reason could there be that these finite,
ephemeral things exist in the midst of nothing,
things that could never add up to the absolute as a
whole or evolve into it? But, on the other hand,
if there is an absolute being, and if this being is
sufficient unto itself, it is almost more mysterious
why there should exist something else. Only a
philosophy of freedom and love can account for
our existence, though not unless it also interprets
the essence of finite being in terms of love. In
terms of love—and not, in the final analysis, in
terms of consciousness, or spirit, or knowledge, or
power, or desire, or usefulness. . . . A light breaks
on the constitution of being itself, . . . insofar as it
subsists in no other way than in the "refusal-to-
cling-to-itself", in the emptying of itself into the
finite and concrete, while finite entities in turn are
able to receive and retain it, as it is in itself, only as
that which does not hold onto itself. Finite beings
are thus trained by it in giving themselves away in

love. One's consciousness, one's self-possession and
possession of being, can grow only and precisely to
the extent that one breaks out of being in and for
oneself in the act of communication, in exchange,
and in human and cosmic *sympatheia*.

Hans Urs von Balthasar
Love Alone Is Credible, 143–44[1]

Hans Urs von Balthasar (1905–1988), the brilliant Roman
Catholic theologian from Switzerland, has been called a
"new Father of the Church"[2] and "a doctor of the Church
for the postmodern age".[3] His theological masterpiece (a
fifteen-volume trilogy regarding beauty, goodness, and
truth) has been referred to as "perhaps the high-point of
twentieth-century Catholic theology".[4] Over fifty years
ago, Karl Rahner, S.J.—despite having some significant
differences from Balthasar[5]—predicted that his theology

---

[1] I have occasionally added bracketed ([ ]) words or phrases to some of
the quotations used in this book for the sake of clarity. I have also italicized
certain words or phrases in some of the quotations in order to emphasize
specific points and have noted the places where I have done so. Within the
text itself, citations for quotations drawn from Balthasar's works will generally
omit the author's name for the sake of brevity. The title of the work from
which the quotation is taken will be listed, followed by the page number, to
assist the reader who would like to pursue further reading regarding specific
quotations or topics. A bibliography providing complete information for each
of Balthasar's publications from which quotations are drawn can be found at
the back of this book. Citations from works other than those by Balthasar will
name the author(s).

[2] Henri Cardinal de Lubac, cited in Angelo Scola, *Hans Urs von Balthasar: A
Theological Style* (Grand Rapids, Mich.: Eerdmans, 1995), 14.

[3] Aidan Nichols, O.P., *Scattering the Seed* (Washington, D.C.: Catholic University
of America Press, 2006), vii.

[4] Aidan Nichols, O.P., *A Key to Balthasar* (Grand Rapids, Mich.: Baker Academic,
2011), 1.

[5] See Hans Urs von Balthasar, *Engagement with God*, trans. R. John Halliburton
(San Francisco: Ignatius Press, 2008).

would exert a growing influence with the passage of time: "Much more of the seed that [Balthasar] has strewn in the field of the Church will sprout than what we see now.... Perhaps the effectiveness of such a theology inevitably takes longer than our impatience is ready to tolerate."[6] Time has begun to bear out Rahner's prediction. Balthasar's theology has already yielded a significant impact, in part via his influence on Saint John Paul II and Pope Emeritus Benedict XVI, both of whom have offered high praise for Balthasar and his work,[7] but also through his influence on new generations of theologians (as indicated by the growing number of dissertations and scholarly publications focusing on Balthasar's work) and on a growing number of laypeople who have begun to read more of his writings.

Rather than losing some of their relevance over time, as happens with the work of so many thinkers and writers, Balthasar's writings have actually *increased* in relevance as Western society has become more secularized (that is, as Western society has increasingly moved religion to the margins of society, relegating it to the realm of private beliefs and preferences and attempting to exclude it entirely from public discourse) and more individualistic, with a seemingly ever-increasing emphasis on the egocentric pursuit of *having* (more pleasure, more money, more power, more status, etc.) as the path to happiness and human fulfillment. We live in a time in which many

---

[6] Karl Rahner, "Hans Urs von Balthasar", in *Civitas* 1965, p. 604, cited in Jeffrey Ames Kay, *Theological Aesthetics: The Role of Aesthetics in the Theological Method of Hans Urs von Balthasar* (Bern: Herbert Lang, 1975), viii.

[7] See John Paul II, Address at the Conferral of the International Paul VI Prize to Hans Urs von Balthasar (June 23, 1984); Joseph Cardinal Ratzinger, "Homily at the Funeral Liturgy for Hans Urs von Balthasar", *Communio: International Catholic Review* 15, no. 4 (1988): 512; Benedict XVI, Message for the Centenary of the Birth of Father Hans Urs von Balthasar (October 6, 2005).

people seem to have lost their awareness of God, their understanding of even a small fragment of the inexpressible significance of Jesus Christ for the human race, their understanding of some of the most important aspects of human existence (including the nature of genuine love, happiness, freedom, and meaning), and their sense of the beautiful, the good, and the true. Balthasar has much of value to say to our world with regard to all of these issues and many more. In this book, we will focus on Balthasar's profound insights regarding the nature of love, a topic that lies at the center of his theology.

When I first started reading Balthasar's writings in my mid forties, I was immediately drawn to his work, in part because of the boldness and confidence with which he raises (and answers!) the "big" questions of human existence, the "existential" questions that I had been pondering for most of my life: Why is there something rather than nothing? Why are we all here? Why am *I*, in particular, here? What is life all about? Is there any ultimate meaning or purpose to life? How can we attain ultimate happiness? How can we attain ultimate freedom?

For Balthasar (and I am firmly convinced that he is right about this), the answers to all of these questions revolve, in one way or another, around *love*. Balthasar's theology is a theology of love. Love lies at the center of Balthasar's writing because love lies at the center of life, indeed, at the center of *being*. As Peter Henrici, S.J., has observed, it is only when we come to see being itself as love that the various facets of Balthasar's theology coalesce into a single, unified form.[8]

---

[8] Peter Henrici, S.J., "The Philosophy of Hans Urs von Balthasar", in *Hans Urs von Balthasar: His Life and Work*, ed. David L. Schindler (San Francisco: Ignatius Press, 1991), 167.

I chose the quotation that opens this introduction from among many others that I could have used because this passage captures the cosmic scope of Balthasar's writing and some of the key themes of his theology. Numerous philosophers have asserted that the most fundamental philosophical question is "Why is there something rather than nothing?" Balthasar, relying on Christian revelation, provides the most persuasive, and the most beautiful, answer to this question of any of the thinkers that I have ever read. As he notes above, "Only a philosophy of freedom and love can account for our existence, though not unless it also interprets the essence of finite being in terms of love. In terms of love—and not, in the final analysis, in terms of consciousness, or spirit, or knowledge, or power, or desire, or usefulness."

There *is* an "absolute being" (i.e., God), and the essence of that absolute being is love. Not power, not knowledge, but love. God *is* "sufficient unto himself" (i.e., God does not need the world in order to be God, nor does God need the world in order to be love), but God, purely out of divine love and freedom, chose to "empty himself into the finite and concrete", that is, to create the entire cosmos so that all of creation (including us human beings) could share in the divine life and love of God. God reveals to us that his essence, and therefore the essence of being itself, is self-giving love. Being, life, does not "cling to itself", but rather gives itself away in love. We were created to share forever in this dynamic movement of love, to open ourselves up to receive the gift of love and to pass the gift of love on to others. As Balthasar so aptly expresses it, "The meaning of the world is love."[9]

[9] Hans Urs von Balthasar, *Heart of the World*, trans. Erasmo S. Leiva (San Francisco: Ignatius Press, 1979), 203.

However, because love is genuine only if freely given and freely received, God gives us the freedom to choose whether to open our hearts and minds to love. Life is a great drama, a "grand school of love"[10] in which our ultimate destiny and the fulfillment of our deepest desires, including our desire for ultimate happiness, meaning, and freedom as well as our desire for beauty, goodness, and truth, hinge on our decision of whether to say Yes or No to love. We can choose to remain within our self-centered, self-enclosed egos, or we can break out of our finitude and into the "immeasurable spaces of freedom",[11] into the infinite spaces of the divine life of God, which is an eternal circulation of love.

A brief note on the purpose of this book

This book was written in the hope of making Balthasar's profound insights regarding the nature of love more accessible to a wider audience of readers and to encourage meditation and reflection upon those insights. Balthasar was a highly gifted theologian, but the sheer volume of his writings can be somewhat daunting (one scholar has estimated that Balthasar's output runs to "several tens of thousands" of pages).[12] In preparation for writing this book, I read nearly everything that I could lay my hands on by Balthasar, carefully selecting only the most illuminating and thought-provoking passages regarding love for inclusion in the present volume. In my commentary, I have tried to provide some context for the selected passages and to draw some connections among Balthasar's most important

---

[10] Ibid., 25.

[11] Ibid., 144.

[12] Melanie Susan Barrett, *Love's Beauty at the Heart of the Christian Moral Life: The Ethics of Catholic Theologian Hans Urs von Balthasar* (Lewiston, Australia: Edwin Mellen Press, 2009), 11.

ideas, but the main focus of the book is meant to be on Balthasar's words, not mine. As such, this book may best be read in a slow, meditative fashion, perhaps reading only a section or two at a time and pausing frequently to reflect deeply on the insights that Balthasar shares with us. Reading Balthasar has significantly enhanced my own understanding of the nature of love; my hope is that you will find this to be true for yourself as well.

Part I

The Eternal Circulation of Love

You will experience ... the sheer joy of the
divine life, which consists in being a closed
circuit of endlessly flowing love.
Heart of the World, 213

Reality, Which Is Love

Love is the ultimate reality—not a random swirl of atoms (as materialists of various stripes have claimed), not power (Nietzsche), not knowledge (Hegel), but *love*—this is the claim that lies at the heart of Balthasar's theology:

> [Love] is the quintessence of all reality!
> *Prayer*, 218

> Reality, which is love, does not "puff itself up" (1 Cor 13:14).
> *You Have Words of Eternal Life*, 38

The essence of life, of being itself, is love:

> The core of being consists in love.
> *Theo-Logic I: Truth of the World*, 225

> Love is ... the depth and height, the length and breadth of being itself.
> *Love Alone Is Credible*, 145

Indeed, Balthasar asserts that love is the ultimate meaning of life:

> The meaning of being consists in love.
> *Theo-Logic I: Truth of the World*, 111

The meaning of the world is love.
Heart of the World, 203

Why is there something rather than nothing? For the sake of love. What is life all about? Love. Why are we all here? To learn how to love, so that we might share as fully as possible in the divine life of God, which is a life of love. *That* is where we will find our ultimate happiness, freedom, purpose, and peace.

2

A Closed Circuit of
Endlessly Flowing Love

Balthasar bases his claim that love is "the quintessence of all reality" on the Christian proclamation that "God is love" (1 Jn 4:8). God is the ultimate reality; the essence of God is love; therefore, the essence of ultimate reality is love.

The little three-word phrase "God is love" is one of the most profound statements ever uttered by human beings. Balthasar refers to it as "the sentence that supports the whole of the Christian message".[1] For some people, however, the phrase "God is love" has become so familiar as to have become almost trite; they may acknowledge that it is true in the abstract, but it is not a truth that they allow to impact their daily lives in any significant way: " 'God is love' sounds nice, but it doesn't pay the bills"—this seems to be the attitude of some people. Other people reject the claim that "God is love" entirely. Balthasar invites both groups of people, in fact, all of us, to consider (or reconsider) the profound meaning and implications of the claim that "God is love". If the ultimate reality is love, then "this changes everything", as a popular phrase puts it. How so? We will be answering that question throughout this

---

[1] Hans Urs von Balthasar, *Epilogue*, trans. Edward T. Oakes (San Francisco: Ignatius Press, 2004), 95.

book, but perhaps the best place to start is with Balthasar's description of the nature of love itself, which is a lot different from, and much more demanding (but also infinitely more fulfilling) than, what most people think love is. Here are several passages in which Balthasar defines love:

> The essence of love is the giving of self.
> *The Christian State of Life*, 162

> Love is the selfless communication
> of what is mine and the selfless
> welcoming of the other in myself.
> *Theo-Logic I: Truth of the World*, 123

> [Love] lies in both giving and receiving
> both the gift and the giver.
> *Theo-Drama II: The Dramatis Personae: Man in God*, 258

I have found it helpful to combine these statements and to express Balthasar's definition of love as follows:

> *Love is the selfless gift of self, given and received.*

What a profound and beautiful definition of love—and an extremely challenging one, too! So if I claim to love someone, it means that I have to be willing to give of my very self to that person and that I also have to be willing to open myself up to receive that other person's proffered gift of self. This conception of love is a lot more demanding than many people's idea of love, which might go no farther than warm feelings toward someone, a strong liking for someone, wishing someone well, etc. Those are all well and good, but Balthasar would assert that they do not go far enough. To capture more fully the depth of what Balthasar means when he refers to love, here are two more pithy phrases from him on the subject of love:

[Love is] self-surrender.
Theo-Drama II: The Dramatis Personae: Man in God, 256

Love is life that pours itself forth.
Heart of the World, 25

How many of us who claim to love someone else are prepared to "surrender" ourselves to that person, much less pour out our very lives for that person? Where does Balthasar get all of this? How does he know so much about the nature of love? From God's revelation, in Jesus Christ, that the essence of the divine life is love and that divine love consists in the selfless gift of self, given and received. Based on that revelation, Balthasar has written some profound descriptions of the divine life as an eternal exchange of the gift of self, referring to the dynamism of the divine life as the eternal circulation or flow of love among the three Persons of the Holy Trinity: Father, Son (Jesus Christ), and Holy Spirit:

[God's] trinitarian life ... is an interminable flowing of the Divine Persons from one another to one another and in one another— an ever actual self-giving.
Christian Meditation, 95

The Father's act of self-giving by which, throughout all created space and time, he pours out the Son is the definitive revealing of the trinitarian act itself in which the "Persons" are God's "relations", forms of absolute self-giving and loving fluidity.
New Elucidations, 119

[God the Father] is absolute love in himself, because, as eternal Father, he is perpetually

begetting the Son whom he loves alone and
who in turn makes himself totally available
to the Father in eternal admiration and the
gift of himself, and ... an eternal exchange
of love between Father and Son takes
place in the Holy Spirit.

Explorations in Theology III: Creator Spirit, 355

God is pure selflessness, the self-giving
of Father to Son, of Son to Father,
of the Spirit to Father and Son.

You Crown the Year with Your Goodness, 179–80

Balthasar uses several striking images related to the "circulation" or "flow" of love to illustrate God the Father's essence as self-giving love, describing the Father as a "flowing wellspring", a "bottomless spring", and the "primordial fountain". Giving himself away in love is not just something the Father *does*; it is what he *is*: God the Father *is* the giving away of self:

Jesus' words indicate that this fruitful self-
surrender by the primal Origin [God the Father]
has neither beginning nor end: It is a perpetual
occurrence in which essence and activity
coincide. Herein lies the most unfathomable
aspect of the Mystery of God: that what is
absolutely primal is no statically self-contained and
comprehensible reality, but one that exists solely
in dispensing itself: a flowing wellspring with no
holding-trough beneath it.... In the pure act of
self-pouring-forth, God the Father is his self, or, if
one wishes, a "person" (in a transcending way).

Credo, 30–31

The Father *is* this act of begetting; he is not on
this side of the Word or above it, a self-contained
God who decided at some time to reproduce
himself. In his innermost principle, God is a
bottomless spring that *is*, in that it gives.
Explorations in Theology III: Creator Spirit, 105

[God the Father is] the primordial fountain,
the source of self-giving love whose
eternal tradition is to hand itself over.
Explorations in Theology V: Man Is Created, 371

Thought's incapacity to exhaust God is one
with its incapacity to exhaust the mystery of
the Father, who was never a self-enclosed, all-
knowing, and all-powerful person, but one
whose identity, from all eternity, was to dispossess
himself in favor of the Son and, that not being
enough, to give himself over yet again, this
time with and through the Son, to the Spirit.
Maintaining itself throughout is what is
essentially divine: the giving over of self.
Theo-Logic II: Truth of God, 137

God the Father is so completely the gift of self that he gives
every aspect of his divine self away in begetting the Son,
except for the only thing he cannot give away, which is his
status as Father or the "unoriginate Origin":[2]

The Father gives the Son everything
except his paternity.
Theo-Logic II: Truth of God, 148

[2] Hans Urs von Balthasar, *Explorations in Theology*, vol. 5, *Man Is Created*,
trans. Adrian Walker (San Francisco: Ignatius Press, 2014), 172.

The Invisible One [God the Father] holds nothing
back when he hands over his prerogatives to the
Lamb [the Son]; he reserves nothing to himself.
Theo-Drama IV: The Action, 52

Insofar as he is the primal source of everything,
"Father", he gives his all, from all eternity, to
his Son, and the absolute bliss of both of them
is to give themselves to each other in return
in the Holy Spirit, who is God as pure gift.
You Crown the Year with Your Goodness, 28

This last quotation draws a connection between self-
giving love and "bliss", a connection that is central to
Balthasar's theology and that provides the answer to the
question of how we attain ultimate happiness: *our ultimate
happiness lies in participating in the eternal circulation of love
that is the divine life*:

You will experience ... the sheer joy of
the divine life, which consists in being a
closed circuit of endlessly flowing love.
Heart of the World, 213

"A closed circuit of endlessly flowing love"—what a beautiful image of the nature of God and hence of ultimate
reality! And how wonderful, and (almost) unbelievable,
that God wants all human beings, indeed, the entire cosmos, to join in this circulation of love forever! *That* is what
life is all about!

This relationship [between God and the
cosmos] is a *circulation* that is included in
the infinite circulation of the Trinity.
Explorations in Theology IV: Spirit and Institution, 40

The infinite [God] and the finite subjects
[human beings] do not simply remain
alongside each other; they live in a
"fluidity" flowing into one another.

Explorations in Theology II: Spouse of the Word, 301

Worldly being is destined to be harbored
in Divine Being, worldly time in God's
eternally moved eternity, worldly space in
the infinite spaces of God, worldly becoming,
not in an immobile Divine Being, but in the
eternal eventfulness of divine life.

Theo-Logic II: Truth of God, 84

The constantly repeated [theme of] "flowing"
refers not only to the animated, circling
unity of life within the Godhead but equally
to the overflowing of this life into the world,
drawing all who believe and love into this
torrent of trinitarian life.[3]

Theo-Drama V: The Last Act, 434

This, then, is why Balthasar referred to God's Trinity as
"the first key to the meaning of existence":[4] the fact that
God's essence is a circulation of love among the three
Persons of the Holy Trinity makes self-giving love the
ultimate reality. God's invitation to all of us to share in
that divine circulation of love forever is an invitation to

---

[3] In this passage, Balthasar is referring to descriptions of the divine life written by three medieval mystics (Mechthild von Magdeburg, Gertrude, and Mechthild von Hackeborn), but his statement applies equally well to his own theology.

[4] Hans Urs von Balthasar, *Convergences: To the Source of Christian Mystery*, trans. E. A. Nelson (San Francisco: Ignatius Press, 1983), 140.

experience the ongoing, ever-increasing fulfillment of our deepest desires, including our desire for happiness, meaning, and freedom as well as our desire for beauty, goodness, and truth, as we shall see in parts 4 and 5 of this book.

3

Blood Circulating in the
Body of the Cosmic Christ

When Balthasar asserts that God's Trinity is "the first key to the meaning of existence", he goes on to say that Christology is the second key.[1] This is because Jesus Christ not only reveals to us that the nature of God (and therefore the nature of ultimate reality) is self-giving love; Jesus is also God's self-gift to the world, who opens up for us the opportunity to participate in the eternal circulation of love that constitutes God's divine life.[2] Balthasar's theology is thus both thoroughly Trinitarian and thoroughly Christocentric. As we shall see in the remainder of this book, almost everything that Balthasar has to say about love (and, indeed, about any other topic of profound importance, such as happiness, meaning, freedom, beauty, goodness, truth, etc.) flows from (1) the nature of the Trinitarian God; and/or (2) the Incarnation, life, and Passion (suffering, death, Resurrection, and Ascension) of Jesus Christ.

---

[1] Hans Urs von Balthasar, *Convergences: To the Source of Christian Mystery*, trans. E. A. Nelson (San Francisco: Ignatius Press, 1983), 140.

[2] The way in which Jesus opens up the divine life to us (and, in fact, to all of creation) via his Incarnation and Passion will be discussed in chapter 16 of this book ("The Goodness of Being: Being Gives Itself").

Here are some of the passages in which Balthasar describes Jesus as the revelation of the divine nature, and, thus, the nature of being itself, as self-giving love:

The trinitarian love that is the essence of all being
... has become visible in Jesus Christ.
Theo-Logic III: The Spirit of Truth, 438

It is only on the basis of Jesus Christ's own
behavior and attitude that we can distinguish such
a plurality [of Divine Persons] in God. Only in
him is the Trinity opened up and made accessible.
Theo-Drama III: The Dramatis Personae:
The Person in Christ, 508

Th[e] primal image of God is Christ, who
knows not desire but is pure self-giving.
Light of the Word, 226

The mind of Christ [is] the spirit of
perfect self-giving.
You Crown the Year with Your Goodness, 274

Jesus Christ is God's loving gift of self to the world; it is Jesus who opens up for us the opportunity to participate in the divine life of God:

Christian revelation is in the first place God's
self-manifestation and self-giving to man
in Jesus Christ and in the Holy Spirit.
A Short Primer for Unsettled Laymen, 70–71

[The] Yes of Mary opens the way to the
ultimate, unreserved, and unqualified self-giving
of God to the world [in Jesus Christ].
Who Is a Christian?, 70

God the Father opens up his heart toward us and toward all of his creation in Jesus Christ, especially in the piercing of Jesus' heart on the Cross (Jn 19:34), which gives us access to the Father's heart and, hence, to the divine life:

[The heart of God] is ... the very center
of God as he opens himself up to man.
Heart of the World, 14

It is the heart of God himself that is laid
open here [in the piercing of Jesus' heart
on the Cross] (for Jesus' heart cannot be
separated from the Father's heart and
the Spirit's heart). The very last that
God can offer up flows out.
Light of the Word, 206

Pierced, the Son's heart gives access to the
Father's heart, and from the wound flows
the Spirit of both for the world.
Light of the Word, 93

The opening of the Heart [of Jesus] is
the handing over of what is most intimate
and personal for the use of all. All may
enter the open, emptied space.
Heart of the World (Preface), 16

[Jesus] is our invitation and initiation
into the mystery of God's heart.
You Crown the Year with Your Goodness, 250

The circuit of love between God and
man is completed in Christ.
You Have Words of Eternal Life, 192

> [Jesus] wants to draw [everyone] into
> the fluid, eternal stream of love that
> circulates between Father and Son.
> *You Crown the Year with Your Goodness*, 173

This is what we were made for: we were made for love.
That is why we are here. We are meant to dwell forever
within the divine life of love. God is love, and we were
made in God's image, in the image of love:

> Insofar as we are [God's] creatures, the
> seed of love lies dormant within us
> as the image of God (*imago*).
> *Love Alone Is Credible*, 76

> God ... infused into [us] a longing for true
> love, so as to draw [us] to it (Jn 6:44).
> *The Glory of the Lord I: Seeing the Form*, 211

Balthasar cites passages from the writings of Saint Cath-
erine of Siena and Julian of Norwich that describe us as
being made out of love and for love:

> [God speaking to Saint Catherine of Siena:] "The
> soul cannot live without love. She always wants
> to love something because love is the stuff she is
> made out of, and through love I created her."
> *The Glory of the Lord V: The Realm of Metaphysics
> in the Modern Age*, 95

> [Julian of Norwich writes] "he has made
> everything which is made for love."
> *The Glory of the Lord V: The Realm of
> Metaphysics in the Modern Age*, 86

Or, as Balthasar himself puts it,

> Love is the watermark in the parchment of our
> existence. It is to love's melody that our limbs
> respond.
> *Heart of the World*, 27

> Man is naturally structured to be able to
> open himself and to be open to others. . . .
> When he opens himself in truth and is open
> in truth to others, he is not complying with
> some heteronomous requirement but
> with the law of his own being.
> *Theo-Logic I: Truth of the World*, 121

> To close ourselves off is to go against the
> very law of being that underpins us.
> *You Crown the Year with Your Goodness*, 149

> Whoever loves is obeying the impulse of
> life in time; whoever refuses to love is
> struggling (uselessly) against the current.
> *Heart of the World*, 27

In a beautiful passage from *Heart of the World* (my favorite book by Balthasar), Balthasar describes human beings as drops of blood flowing forever out to other human beings in love and then back into the heart of God, all within the Body of Christ. I would like to quote this passage at some length, in part because of its poetic quality, and in part because it touches upon several Balthasarian themes regarding love upon which we will be meditating in this book:

> This is the body [the Body of Christ] in which
> you are to flow, letting yourself be driven ever

anew as a drop through red ventricles and throbbing arteries. In this circulation you will experience both the futility of your resistance as you put up a struggle and the power of the muscle that drives you forward. You will experience the anguish of the creature that must humble and lose itself, but also the sheer joy of the divine life, which consists in being a closed circuit of endlessly flowing love. Washed along on the tide of the sacred Blood, you will encounter all things as pebble knocks against pebble in the cataracts of a mountain stream, but also in the way handsome sailboats cross on the gently changing landscape of a royal river. Pushed along in the detachment of dark solitude, you will learn to know that the communion of all beings among themselves is their contact with one another and their selfhood within the flowing channels of that Body. Thus related to all things and all natures, you will at last be able to commune also with yourself, and by way of self-forgetfulness—that lengthiest of all detours—you will be brought to the festive Table of Offerings upon which you will find yourself lying as a stranger who is given to himself as a new gift. Expelled from the Heart, out to all the members of that colossal Body, you will undertake a voyage longer than any of Columbus'. But just as the earth rounds itself off into a ball, so, too, do the veins make a return to the Heart and love goes out and comes back eternally. Slowly you will master the rhythm, and

you will no longer grow fearful when the Heart
drives you out into emptiness and death, for then
you will know that that is the shortest route to be
admitted again into [the] fullness of delight. And
when it pushes you away from itself, then you
should know that this is your mission: being sent
away from the Son, you yourself repeat the way
of the Son, away from the Father and out to the
world. And your way to remote places, where the
Father is not, is the way of God himself, who goes
out from himself, abandons himself, lets himself
fall, leaves himself in the lurch. But this going
out of the Son is also the going out of the Spirit
from the Father and the Son, and the Spirit is the
return of the Son to the Father. At the outermost
margin of existence, at the furthest shore, where
the Father is invisible and wholly hidden, there
the Son breathes out his Spirit, whispers it into
the chaos and the darkness, and the Spirit of God
hovers over the waters. And hovering in the
Spirit, the Son turns back to the Father glorified,
and you along with him and in him, and the
departure and the return are one and the same.
Nothing any longer exists outside of this
one and only flowing life.
Heart of the World, 212–14

The Body of Christ is the space within which all of us are
intended to dwell forever in the divine life of God, the
Body within which we are to join in the eternal circulation of love. As Balthasar so eloquently expresses it, we

were created to be the "blood circulating in the Body of the cosmic Christ".[3] *That* is our intended destiny: to dwell forever within the heart of God, within the eternal circulation of love that is the divine life. That is where we will find our ultimate fulfillment. And that is why Balthasar, echoing Scripture, insists that our ultimate destiny hinges on a decision for or against Jesus:

> Every man's final destiny will be determined
> by his attitude to Jesus (Mk 8:38).
> *Theo-Drama III: The Dramatis Personae:*
> *The Person in Christ,* 27

Balthasar describes human existence as a "theo-drama":[4] our life is a drama in which our ultimate destiny (including the fulfillment of our deepest desires for happiness, meaning, freedom, beauty, goodness, and truth) will be determined by our free decision of whether to accept or reject God's offer of a share in the divine life of love in Jesus Christ, who entered into human history, indeed, became one of us (the "theo" part of the theo-drama), to make such a destiny possible for us.

Balthasar sometimes frames this decision, the most important decision each of us will ever make, in terms of a choice between remaining within the cramped, finite confines of our own egos or stepping out into the infinite spaces of God's love and freedom. He also frames this decision in terms of choosing whether to open or close our hearts to love. These themes will arise repeatedly in

---

[3] Hans Urs von Balthasar, *Heart of the World*, trans. Erasmo S. Leiva (San Francisco: Ignatius Press, 1979), 212.

[4] Hans Urs von Balthasar, *Theo-Drama: Theological Dramatic Theory*, 5 vols. (San Francisco: Ignatius Press, 1988–1998).

the remainder of this book, but we will especially return to them in the final part of this book. For now, let us turn our attention to a deeper reflection upon the nature of the love to which we are called to give a definitive Yes or No.

Part II

The Selfless Gift of Self, Given and Received

The essence of love is the giving of self.
The Christian State of Life, 162

Love is the selfless communication
of what is mine and the selfless
welcoming of the other in myself.
Theo-Logic I: Truth of the World, 123

[Love] lies in both giving and receiving
both the gift and the giver.
Theo-Drama II: The Dramatis Personae: Man in God, 258

As you will recall, I combined the above passages from Balthasar and restated his definition of love as *the selfless gift of self, given and received*, back in chapter 2. In this next part of the book, we will be meditating in more detail upon the nature of love as described by Balthasar. I will structure our discussion around the three elements contained in this definition. We will start with the heart of love, which is the gift of self (chapter 4), move on to the *exchange* of the gift of self ("given and received") (chapter 5), and then conclude this part of the book with the aspect of love that many people find to be the most difficult to live out: the *selflessness* that is an essential component of genuine love (chapter 6).

4

The Gift of Self

a. *Hingabe*

[Love is] self-surrender.
Theo-Drama II: The Dramatis Personae: Man in God, 256

Balthasar uses a variety of images within his massive *oeuvres* to depict the nature of love as self-gift; in this section and the next, I would like for us to reflect on two of the more vivid images that he uses: *Hingabe* (a German word meaning to "surrender" or to "hand oneself over" to another) and eucharistic self-giving.

Balthasar apparently thought that the motif of *Hingabe* or "surrender" was particularly descriptive of the nature of self-gift required by genuine love, because he uses this motif over and over throughout his writings, so much so that Aidan Nichols, O.P., an expert on Balthasar's theology, referred to this motif as Balthasar's "beloved *Hingabe*".[1] For Balthasar, love is self-surrender because the essence of *God* is self-surrender:

> And it is precisely in this infinite surrender and
> self-renunciation, in this absolute preference of

---

[1] Aidan Nichols, O.P., *Scattering the Seed* (Washington, D.C.: Catholic University of America Press, 2006), 163.

the Thou to the I, that the life of the Trinity
consists; for it is a life in which the Persons can
be conceived only "relatively", that is, through
one another. The Father only is, as he who
generates the Son, he who surrenders and pours
himself out in the Son; and the Son is, only as
he who utterly surrenders himself to the Father,
acknowledging himself to be the Father's glory
and image; the Spirit is, only as witnessing and
expressing the love between the Father and
the Son, and proceeding from them.

Explorations in Theology I: The Word Made Flesh, 169

This love that has its source in the Father is,
initially, the Father himself (since, as Father, he is
nothing other than the pure surrender of himself;
the Father does not "have" love, he "is" love).

Theo-Logic III: The Spirit of Truth, 441

In the Father there is nothing beyond this
eternal "Yes" to the Son, nothing he keeps
to himself and does not share with the Son;
the Son dwells in the Father's absolute,
boundless self-surrender to him; he is the
result of this self-surrender; indeed, he *is* it.

You Crown the Year with Your Goodness, 124

God is always the one who has lovingly
surrendered himself in freedom.

Explorations in Theology IV: Spirit and Institution, 340

Absolute love ... consists in pure self-surrender.

Explorations in Theology IV: Spirit and Institution, 435

Thus, God's essence consists in the reciprocal self-surrender
of Father, Son, and Holy Spirit to each other in the eternal

exchange of love that is the life of the Trinity. God also freely surrenders himself to all of creation in the Incarnation, death, and Resurrection of his Son and invites us to participate in the divine life by joining in the dynamic of self-surrender in our relationship with God and neighbor.

For many people, the language of "surrender" can be somewhat unappealing initially, because surrender seems to connote weakness, even powerlessness, but as Balthasar points out in many different passages, true power lies in self-surrendering love rather than self-assertion:

> ... the Trinitarian archetype, in which the highest power shows itself in the highest self-surrender....
>
> *Explorations in Theology V: Man Is Created*, 250

> [God the Father's] almightiness can be none other than that of a surrender which is limited by nothing—what could surpass the power of bringing forth a God "equal in nature", that is, equally loving and equally powerful, not another God but an other in God.... It is therefore essential ... to see the unimaginable power of the Father in the force of his self-surrender, that is, of his love, and not, for example, in his being able to do this or that as he chooses.
>
> *Credo*, 31

> The triune love of God has power only in the form of surrender (and in the vulnerability and powerlessness that is part of the essence of that surrender).
>
> *Explorations in Theology IV: Spirit and Institution*, 435

> God is not, in the first place, "absolute power", but "absolute love", and his sovereignty manifests

itself not in holding on to what is its own but
in its abandonment—all this in such a way that
this sovereignty displays itself in transcending
the opposition, known to us from the world,
between power and impotence.
Mysterium Paschale, 28

[Mary's] maternal concern is to teach everyone
to have the mind of Christ, the spirit of perfect
self-giving, which is ultimately the most powerful
thing in the world, more powerful than all powers
and authorities, for they are all subordinate to it.
You Crown the Year with Your Goodness, 274

Where is life more conscious of its potency
than in the pleasure of giving itself away?
Must we not say that life is never more alive
than when it gives itself up and dies over into
the other?... Man is finite, but he is capable
of giving himself infinitely.
Explorations in Theology V: Man Is Created, 360

Strength is located precisely in love.
Light of the Word, 353

First and foremost, we are to surrender ourselves or hand
ourselves over in love to *God*, in loving response to the
loving self-surrender of God to us in Jesus Christ and in
our best effort to imitate Jesus' admittedly inimitable self-
surrender to God the Father:

[Saint John the Evangelist] can, without further
ado, read the life and death of the Son of God,
the surrender of his life for the life of the

world, as being the love of God himself, a
love which teaches us to respond with our
own love by means of our unconditional
and loving self-surrender to it.
The Glory of the Lord I: Seeing the Form, 572

Jesus lived day by day, hour by hour, in an
attitude of self-surrender to the Father.
You Crown the Year with Your Goodness, 232

This humanity of Jesus is expropriated for
God in an unparalleled way and is therein
the archetype of surrender to God, at
once inimitable and, nevertheless,
to be imitated by all men.
Theo-Logic II: Truth of God, 283

Jesus, in his self-surrender to the world, opens up to us
the divine life of love, and the Holy Spirit guides us into a
participation in this divine life of self-surrender via his own
surrender to anyone who "receives his testimony":

The milieu of love between Father and
Son is opened up in the Son as a result of
his self-surrender to the world; so too the
Spirit's introduction into this milieu of love,
which is truth, is also the Spirit's self-surrender
to the person who receives his testimony....
So his "leading into all truth" is initially
something quite different from the imparting
of information; rather, he leads us from inner
participation into inner participation.
Theo-Logic III: The Spirit of Truth, 74

Created being ... owes its ... vocation of
self-surrender to the Spirit, who is the
embodiment, in God, of love's generosity.
Theo-Drama V: The Last Act, 76

What is required is not that we relinquish our
"I" but that we hand ourselves over to the
absolute "Thou" of our Origin, who
challenges us and seeks to win our love.
You Crown the Year with Your Goodness, 170

Balthasar draws on some of the writings of the saints in describing our love for God in terms of self-surrender, sometimes equating self-surrender not only with love but also with faith and/or trust in God:

Like [Saint] Paul, the Christian lives an existence
in faith, faith being understood as a living
handing over of self to God. For [Saint] John [the
Evangelist], such self-surrender to the incarnate
Beloved is simply one and the same thing as love.
The Glory of the Lord I: Seeing the Form, 230

Balthasar bases the following statement on Saint John of the Cross' description of love:

Love is the surrender of the whole of
our being to the God we love.
The Glory of the Lord III: Studies in Theological Style:
Lay Styles, 133

Balthasar also approvingly quotes Saint Thérèse of Lisieux's description of her famous "little way of love" as a path of self-surrender:

" 'The little way ... is *the way of spiritual childhood,
the way of trust and total surrender.*' "
Two Sisters in the Spirit, 297

In numerous other passages, Balthasar himself equates self-surrender with love, faith, and/or trust:

Love itself is the surrender of one's entire will and
being through faith, in the conviction that God
merits to be placed first in every respect and is
deserving of total surrender; in a trust, too, that in
its knowledge surpasses all knowledge.
Explorations in Theology I: The Word Made Flesh, 168–69

The faith that the Christian must have
[is] a trusting self-surrender to God, for
the most part unsupported by sight.
Theo-Drama V: The Last Act, 123

... a childlike surrender in trust of all that
we have or are to the love of God.
Engagement with God, 38

In addition to being called to loving self-surrender to
God, we are also called to surrender ourselves in love to
other people. Balthasar does not use the language of self-surrender nearly as much in speaking of loving other people as he does in speaking of loving God, but here is one
such passage, in which Balthasar notes that self-surrender
on behalf of one's neighbor is, in fact, simultaneously a
form of surrender to God:

[Creatures] are to surrender themselves for their
neighbor (whoever he may be); thus, concretely,

> they offer their self-surrender through every
> particular instance to Being in its totality.
> *Theo-Drama V: The Last Act*, 76

Balthasar sometimes draws an analogy between death and the loving self-surrender of God the Father, Son, and Holy Spirit to each other. Handing ourselves over in love to God or neighbor constitutes a form of "death" for us as well.[2] That, of course, is one of the factors that makes loving self-surrender so difficult for us:

> There is an archetype in God of "good death":
> in the unconditional self-surrender of each divine
> hypostasis [Divine Person] to the others.
> *Theo-Logic II: Truth of God*, 83

> The most difficult thing that can be
> asked of man—his self-surrender.
> *The Threefold Garland*, 130

Ultimately, we will all have to surrender ourselves to God at the time of our physical death, either willingly, in a loving handing over of ourselves to God, or else unwillingly. It will be much easier to hand ourselves over to God lovingly in death if we have already been working on loving self-surrender to God during our earthly life. Surrendering ourselves in love to God at death gives a profound significance and meaning to death, integrating death's "victim" into the divine life of loving self-surrender:

> The reality of dying, as the human being's giving
> up of self—this reality has lost its sting (the feeling

[2] Hans Urs von Balthasar, *Theo-Logic: Theological Logical Theory*, vol. 3, *The Spirit of Truth*, trans. Graham Harrison (San Francisco: Ignatius Press, 2005), 241.

that, in the end, "it was all for nothing") and is
drawn up into the process of eternal life. When
the Father surrenders himself unreservedly to
the Son, and when, in turn, the Father and Son
surrender themselves similarly to the Holy Spirit,
do we not find here the archetype of the most
beautiful dying in the midst of eternal life? Is this
final state of "not wanting to be for oneself" not
precisely the prerequisite for the most blessed life?
Into this most living "higher dying" our own
wretched dying is taken up and resolved, so that
everything human—its being saved, its living, its
dying—is thenceforth securely integrated into
a life that no longer knows any limits.

Credo, 59–60

Self-surrender is ultimate; it is the ultimate in
God the Father, in the Son and in the Spirit,
and it is the ultimate in man, too, when he
has reached the end of his crazy path.

Theo-Drama V: The Last Act, 188

Through his loving death for us, Jesus has transformed
physical death into an act of love that we are to imitate at
the time of our own actual death:

Since this love-death of our Lord, death has
taken on a quite different meaning; it can
become for us an expression of our purest
and most living love, assuming that we take it
as a conferred opportunity to give ourselves
unreservedly into the hands of God.

Credo, 54

> Dying, ... undertaken in a Christian spirit,
> is an act of pure self-surrender in which
> we allow ourselves to be taken hence.
> *You Crown the Year with Your Goodness*, 126

Michel de Montaigne (1533–1592), the French essayist, once wrote, "He who would teach men to die would teach them to live."[3] He was on to something there. It is only when we learn to die to self in self-surrendering love for God and neighbor that we first begin to learn how truly to live.

b. Love Is Life that Pours Itself Forth

In addition to the language of self-surrender, Balthasar sometimes uses the motif of "eucharistic self-giving" to express the depth of the self-giving love to which God calls us. "Eucharistic" here refers to the total gift of self found (1) within the life of the Trinity; (2) in Jesus' sacrifice on the Cross for the redemption of the world; and (3) in the sacrament of the Eucharist, in which Jesus breaks open his Body and pours out his Blood as literal food and drink for us so that we can become more fully incorporated into his Body. We, too, are to "break ourselves open and pour ourselves out" in love for God and neighbor, becoming food and drink for them in a metaphorical comparison to the Eucharist. Thus, Balthasar's beautiful expression of love as "life that pours itself forth".[4]

---

[3] *Essays*, I, 20, cited in John Bartlett, *Bartlett's Familiar Quotations* (Boston: Little, Brown, 2002), 152.

[4] Hans Urs von Balthasar, *Heart of the World*, trans. Erasmo S. Leiva (San Francisco: Ignatius Press, 1979), 25.

Balthasar makes direct reference to eucharistic self-giving among the Persons of the Trinity in the following passage:

> In intertrinitary life all the divine hypostases
> [God the Father, the Son, and the Holy
> Spirit] are "eucharistic" food for each other....
> This "losing" of oneself to each other and
> within each other ... is ... a form and
> expression of utmost aliveness.
> *Life Out of Death*, 70

However, most of Balthasar's comments with regard to eucharistic self-giving are focused upon Jesus' pouring out of himself in love for us and upon the way in which this reveals the essence of God and the type of self-giving love to which we are all called:

> [Jesus'] humanity ... comes to share in
> [the divine] glory ... by being finally opened
> to all (in the Eucharist) and drained
> (ultimately, in the opening of his heart).
> *Theo-Drama IV: The Action*, 363

> Christ's body has become finally and definitively
> eucharistic, both since he suffered for all human
> sin and since the mode of being of this body
> has been assimilated to the trinitarian mode
> of being of the ascended Son: its being
> is not for itself but for the other.
> *Theo-Drama V: The Last Act*, 382

> [Jesus] will never gather into himself his
> eucharistic fragmentation in order to be

> at one with himself. Even as the risen Lord he
> lives as the one who has given himself
> and has poured himself out.
> *Elucidations*, 183

Participating in Jesus' eucharistic self-giving is thus one of the ways in which we participate in the life of the Trinity:

> Beholding and inwardly participating in
> the Son in his eucharistic self-giving becomes
> a beholding and a participating in the life of
> the Trinity. For when the Son allows himself
> to be poured out, he directly reveals the love
> of the Father, who manifests himself in
> his Son's *eucharistia*.
> *Theo-Drama V: The Last Act*, 384

In numerous passages, Balthasar specifically emphasizes the necessity for the Church, and for individual Christians, too, to enter into the movement of Jesus' eucharistic self-gift. In these passages, Balthasar sometimes makes reference to the need for us to be willing to make sacrifices and/or to undergo suffering for the sake of love; we will be reflecting upon these particularly challenging aspects of love in more detail in chapter 6, sections d and e.

> [The Church] must, with Christ and through
> him, give to us his Body and his Blood,
> give of herself for the salvation of the world.
> Or—rather, since she is Bride, since Mary
> is her heart—she must consent to being
> given, allow herself to be distributed.
> *To the Heart of the Mystery of Redemption*, 64

The Church cannot celebrate the sacrifice of the
Mass without offering herself to be included in
that sacrifice. She only genuinely receives the
food Jesus offers if she shares his sacrificial mind.

You Crown the Year with Your Goodness, 133

There is something like a eucharistic bloodbath
when [the Church's] own flesh and blood,
too—is she not the body of Christ?—
is food for the life of the world.

Life Out of Death, 79

If the Cross is a sacrifice, or rather the only
perfect sacrifice, and if in the Mass we become
present anew to Christ's work of salvation to
the point of being allowed to receive his Body
that is given up and his Blood that is poured
out, then it should be self-evident that we are
thereby *drawn into* his attitude of self-giving
and thus into *his sacrificial attitude.*

A Short Primer for Unsettled Laymen, 102

Christ's commandment to eat his slaughtered flesh
and to drink his poured-out blood, and to do this
in commemoration of him, does not at all mean
only a cultic-sacramental act. It does indeed mean
this, but not only this. "Do this" means absolutely
also: follow me in this in your life. If I have given
my life for you, then you too should give your
life for the brethren, for the world.

Explorations in Theology II: Spouse of the Word, 509

Everyone who serves is a unique human being,
and the love in his heart is irreplaceable. He

pours his personal love into the great anonymous
whole, and such self-giving—when done
with conscious awareness—is almost like
a death. A sacrificial death.
Who Is a Christian?, 119

The spark of the *"bonum diffusivum sui"* [the
self-diffusiveness of the good] enters into the
man who is privileged to glimpse it and makes
him, too, a person who is unreservedly "poured
out". He becomes the unique point through
which the universal Logos [Jesus] wishes
to communicate himself to everyone.
Theo-Drama II: The Dramatis Personae: Man in God, 32

Balthasar's most explicit use of eucharistic language in discussing self-giving love is often based on the writings of
Origen (ca. 184—ca. 253):

Origen even speaks of an analogy with
the Eucharist: insofar as a man belongs to
Christ, he can be shared out with Christ
as nourishment for the Mystical Body.
Theo-Drama III: The Dramatis Personae:
The Person in Christ, 527–28

Origen ... demands that Christ be made present,
not only through prayer but also through the
gift of one's own life in suffering, something that
[Saint] John [the Evangelist] absolutely demands
of Christians in the imitation of Christ (1 Jn 3:16);
such a capacity of the apostles, of the disciples,
and of every saint who truly makes a gift of

himself, to offer out of his own substance a true
bread and a true wine to his brethren..., can
of course be conceived of meaningfully only
within the Eucharistic self-giving of Christ:
as a mystery of the fruitful Vine.
Explorations in Theology II: Spouse of the Word, 390

[Christians'] existence, their hearts, their prayer
is a loaf in which all should share. Why should
Christians not be permitted to have a share in
the eucharistic mystery? [Balthasar then, in n. 5,
quotes Origen directly:] "And so each person
has the capacity, according to the measure of his
commitment or the purity of his intentions, to be
pure food to his neighbor. Every one of us has a
certain kind of food within him. If it is good and
he draws from it and brings forth good things
from the good treasures of his heart, then
he offers his neighbor a pure food."
Who Is a Christian?, 128–29

[Jesus'] eucharistic attitude must become the
motif of Christian life, a life lived in imitation
of God's love, an imitation that can only
consist in mutual love, compassion, and
forgiveness. Through these the "beloved
children of God" become for each other a
sort of eucharistic nourishment for the
journey—something like food that
unexpectedly materializes for our neighbors
in the middle of the desert of our lives, like
Elijah's piece of bread and jar of water.
Light of the Word, 228

It would not be stretching Balthasar's ideas regarding eucharistic self-giving to assert that we are most fully alive when we are most fully "breaking ourselves open" and "pouring ourselves out" in loving self-gift to God and neighbor, for it is precisely then that we most fully participate in the superabundant, overflowing life of God.

5

Given and Received

a. The Two Movements of Love

Balthasar has referred to the *giving* and the *receiving* of the gift of self as the two "aspects" of love,[1] but in keeping with his use of dynamic terminology to describe the circulation and flow of love within the divine life, between God and creation, and among human beings, I prefer to refer to these two "aspects" of love as the two "movements" of love. I have also coined a new term to refer to the act of giving the gift of self in love in order to facilitate the discussion of, and reflection upon, this movement of love: *donativity*. I derived this word from the Latin word *donare* ("to give"),[2] choosing its particular form to parallel the form of the term that Balthasar frequently uses to refer to the other movement of love: *receptivity*. Thus, the two movements of love can be referred to as donativity and receptivity.

As with almost every other aspect of love that Balthasar discusses, the archetypes for donativity and receptivity are found within the Trinitarian life of God:[3]

---

[1] Hans Urs von Balthasar, *Explorations in Theology*, vol. 5, *Man Is Created*, trans. Adrian Walker (San Francisco: Ignatius Press, 2014), 172.

[2] *The American Heritage Dictionary of the English Language*, 5th ed. (Boston: Houghton Mifflin, 2012), s.v. "donation".

[3] I added italics to some of the quotations in this chapter in order to emphasize the references to one or both of the movements of love.

God's triune vitality contains a *double form*
of loving self-surrender: a purely active
donation, on the one hand, and a passive–active
answering *reception*, on the other. Both forms
are coeternal, and each presupposes the other.
The Father, the unoriginate Origin, *gives*
himself away totally and, in so doing, brings
forth the Son. Accordingly, the Son not only
receives himself passively from all eternity but,
with an equally eternal action, also *gives*
himself, as subsistent gratitude, back to his
Origin. From all eternity ..., then, the
beatitude of the self-giving Father consists
equally in two things at once: in his own
eternal and active deed of *giving* himself away
and in his ("passive") *reception* of the Son's self-
return as (eucharistic) thanksgiving. We could
accordingly understand the Spirit's procession
from the Father and the Son (in line with
Western theology) as a gift flowing from an
activity common to both, an activity that already
includes the *marriage of the two aspects of love*, each
of which is present in its own distinct way.
Explorations in Theology V: Man Is Created, 172

The Spirit, as the spirit of love, rests perfectly
in the self-*giving* of the Father and perfectly
in the *receiving* love of the Son.
You Have Words of Eternal Life, 15

The divine self-*giving* [among God the Father,
Son, and Holy Spirit] becomes the prototype
and archetype of [God's] self-*giving* to the

world and of all the *traditio* ["*handing on*" or
giving of self in love] that flows from it.
Theo-Drama IV: The Action, 53

God is pure selflessness, the self-*giving* of Father to
Son, of Son to Father, of the Spirit to Father and
Son; being filled with God means plunging into
this torrent of selflessness of the life of God, that
is eternally *handing itself over* to the Other in a
never-ending spiral of *giving* and *receiving*.
You Crown the Year with Your Goodness, 179–80

Jesus Christ is the visible revelation and exemplar of this
eternal dynamic of donativity and receptivity that constitutes the divine life:

The Son's form of existence, which makes
him the Son from all eternity ([Jn] 17:5), is
the uninterrupted *reception* of everything that
he is, of his very self, from the Father. It is
indeed this *receiving* of himself which gives
him his "I", his own inner dimension, his
spontaneity, that sonship with which he can
answer the Father in a reciprocal *giving*.
A Theology of History, 30

The Son exists as *receptivity*, gratitude
and *giving-in-return*.
You Crown the Year with Your Goodness, 144

For us human beings, love must begin with receptivity;
we must first receive love from God before we can pass
the divine gift of self-giving love along to others. Some
of us can be reluctant to receive God's gift of himself (out

of such motives as a desire for complete self-sufficiency or autonomy), but as Jesus has shown us, receptivity is actually an aspect of the divine. We are to strive to imitate, not only Jesus' donativity, but also his receptivity:

> Faith means a readiness to *receive* the love of God
> as a gift, as one acknowledges God's deed of
> love, as one permits it to occur to oneself. Such
> *acceptance*, such recognition then becomes the
> innermost ground of the human responding love
> and becomes indeed the initiator of such love.
> *Elucidations*, 74

> Did not each of us have to *receive* love before
> he could even know the meaning of the word?
> If each of us is a wave in the onward-flowing
> stream, do we not owe our identity entirely
> to a source that sustains us? To a spring whose
> uninterrupted self-*gift* awakens in us the
> urge to *hand on the gift* in our turn?
> *Explorations in Theology V: Man Is Created*, 369

> No one simply *gives* without *taking*, if
> only because all *receive* from Christ, and
> everyone's *giving* is nothing but an answer
> to, and an effect of, this *reception*.
> *Mary: The Church at the Source*, 136

In response to God's loving self-gift to us and to the world, we should give ourselves in love to God and neighbor, passing along the divine gift of love:

> The love that is made manifest in God and his
> revelation ... must be implemented ... in both
> directions exemplified by the Son, namely,

toward the Father and, coming from the
Father, toward the world.
Theo-Logic III: The Spirit of Truth, 76

From the beginning, we were a *gift* that you
have *given* us; we *give* everything back to you,
dispose of it according to your will alone.
Explorations in Theology III: Creator Spirit, 542

The person privileged to share in Christ's *radiance*
is more profoundly redeemed than the person
who is merely the *recipient* of these radiant beams.
In the Fullness of Faith, 123

[T]he Christian must always be inwardly
aware that everything he is able to *pass on*
comes from God for the benefit of others.
Light of the Word, 46

In *receiving* ourselves from the primordial source,
we *receive* the power to be a source in communion
with him—the power to *give* ourselves.
Explorations in Theology V: Man Is Created, 371

Insofar as [the Christian] abides by this source
and quenches his own thirst here, he too can
open up the way to this source to others who
likewise thirst, can even through his own
person *give* to others to drink out of this
same source (see Jn 4:14; 7:3ff.).
Engagement with God, 60

[I]t is already *given* to believers, even on
earth, not only to possess the Holy
Spirit but to *"exhale"* the Spirit.
Explorations in Theology IV: Spirit and Institution, 443

> For my grace is always fruitful, and my *gift*
> it is for you to *pass my grace on*. My treasure
> is to be found in prodigality, and only he
> possesses me who *gives* me away.
>
> *Heart of the World*, 83

> [Time] wants you to be more loving. And if
> you were once to follow wholeheartedly the
> law and imperative of your very being, if
> you were once fully yourself, you would live
> solely on this *gift* that flows out to you (this *gift*
> which you yourself are), and you would do this
> by *giving* it away in turn, in holiness without
> having defiled it through possessiveness.
>
> *Heart of the World*, 28–29

In addition to being thoroughly Trinitarian and Christocentric, Balthasar's theology is also highly Marian in character. In the following passages, he holds Mary up to us as
an excellent exemplar of allowing God to insert us into the
divine dynamic of the reception and transmission of love:

> [Mary] does what grace wants, namely, *hands it
> on, gives* it away, pours it out for others. The more
> *receptive* a person is to grace, the more active and
> productive grace becomes in him and he in grace.
>
> *You Crown the Year with Your Goodness*, 273

> If each of God's *gifts* also contains his petition
> and demand that we should *receive* the *gift* and
> *reciprocate* it, it is in Mary that the correspondence
> between *gift* and self-*giving*, *reception* and
> thanks*giving* attains perfection. This makes man

capable of being fruitful along with the eternal
fruitfulness of God, so that out of his completed
self-surrender he can, in turn, form a *gift* and thus
transmit the divine grace further through himself.
Mary-the-Church keeps no grace for herself; she
receives grace in order to *transmit* it. This is what
a mother does. We are the children of Mary's
fruitfulness, and her fruitfulness has been *given*
her that she might *receive* and fulfill the fruitfulness
of her Spouse. And this obliges us, too, ourselves
to be the Church and to become inserted into
this cycle of *reception* and *transmission*.
The Threefold Garland, 137

b. That Person Loves Who Opens Himself Up

An absolutely essential component of receptivity and
donativity, of the giving and receiving of the gift of self
in love, is *openness*, another frequently recurring theme in
Balthasar's writings. One cannot give the gift of self, or
receive the gift of self from others, if one is closed up within
oneself. This is why Balthasar often frames the choice for
or against love as a choice between remaining enclosed
within one's own ego versus stepping outside of one's ego
and into the infinite spaces of the divine love. Once again,
the archetype of openness is found in God:

The divine hypostases [God the Father, Son,
and Holy Spirit] proceed from one another and
thus (including the Father, the Primal Source)
are perfectly open to one another.
Theo-Drama II: The Dramatis Personae: Man in God, 258

The divine hypostases know and interpenetrate
each other to the very same degree that each of
them opens up to the other in absolute freedom.
Theo-Drama II: The Dramatis Personae: Man in God, 259

God is "openness" within the divine life, but God is also
openness toward us and the world through Jesus Christ:

In Christ, God and man, God has
opened himself to the world.
Explorations in Theology I: The Word Made Flesh, 162

God the Father has acted in Jesus Christ
so definitively toward the world that he has
at the same time laid open in him the inmost
parts of his heart, his trinitarian love.
Elucidations, 138

The opening of the Heart [of Jesus Christ
on the Cross] is the handing over of what is
most intimate and personal for the use of all.
All may enter the open, emptied space.
Heart of the World, 16

God is not a sealed fortress, to be attacked
and seized by our engines of war (ascetic
practices, meditative techniques, and the like)
but a house full of open doors, through
which we are invited to walk.
You Crown the Year with Your Goodness, 144

It is not we who flow forth: you [God] are the
stream, the moving breath of love. You are
yourself by being the one who is selfless. The

Persons in you are not fixed points but oscillating
relationships, forms of the gift of self, no
fortresses that one would have to take by
storm, but opennesses: the only one to win
a share in them is the one who abandons
his own fortress and emerges from it.
Explorations in Theology III: Creator Spirit, 538

God created us to be open to love in imitation of the
divine openness:

[Jesus speaking to every human being:]
You would not be my creature if you
had not been created open.
Heart of the World, 143

[O]ur "I" is always bathed in this all-embracing
life [the loving openness of the Trinity];
to close ourselves off is to go against the
very law of being that underpins us.
You Crown the Year with Your Goodness, 149

If we are willing, God will open us up from "both sides"
to participate in the divine love, i.e., in terms of both
receptivity (opening us up to receive God's gift of self to
us) and donativity (opening us up to pass that gift of the
divine life and love on to others):

The turning of "the whole heart" towards God
is the opening of the whole man to him.
Mysterium Paschale, 130

It is only when the innermost heart of a man
is opened that the sun of love can penetrate

into it. *"Fili, praebe mihi cor tuum*, Son,
give me your heart" (Prov 23:26).
Elucidations, 232

[Jesus] was always the Word from the open
God and the Word for open persons. The
Spirit prevents us from closing the
Word by closing our heart to it.
Explorations in Theology III: Creator Spirit, 114

To [the Holy Spirit], the most delicate,
vulnerable, and precious one in God, we
must open ourselves up, without defensiveness,
without thinking that we know better, without
hardening ourselves, so that we may undergo
initiation by him into the Mystery that God
is love.... Through [the Holy Spirit] we
can really learn what, in his view, love is.
Credo, 76

"The Spirit poured out into our hearts" (Rom
5:1–5) ... imbues in us this very inner openness of
the triune God and habituates us to it from both
sides: enabling us to answer God's address and gift
to us in a way worthy of God and to carry within
us God's own disposition [of self-giving love].
Explorations in Theology IV: Spirit and Institution, 440

From the opened Trinity, which is made available
to us in the opened broken heart on the Cross,
there streams forth the tremendous mystery
of everlasting love, and, overwhelmed by it,
the Christian gives his heart to his brother—
boundlessly, even to the point of dying for him.
The Moment of Christian Witness, 123

That person loves who opens himself up
in order to communicate himself.
Heart of the World, 37

Balthasar also discusses the necessity of openness in order
for us to be able to receive, in love, the gift of self offered
to us by others. These passages establish a clear connection
between the receptive movement of love and the openness
that such receptivity requires:

Receptivity means accessibility to another's
being, openness to something other than
the inner dimension of one's own subjectivity,
the possession of windows looking out on
all being and truth. Receptivity signifies the
power to welcome and, so to say, host
another's being in one's own home. It follows
that the more perfectly an entity possesses
itself, the freer it is, the less closed in on itself
it is, and, therefore, the more receptive
it is to everything around it.
Theo-Logic I: Truth of the World, 44–45

Receptivity is thus like a deep, unclosable breach
opened up in the closed circle of being-for-itself.
Only by welcoming things from the outside and
remaining open to them, only by being given
over to the service of what is other than itself, can
man's spirit lay claim to a being of its own.
Theo-Logic I: Truth of the World, 98

We are ourselves by simultaneously making
ourselves a dwelling place for others.
Theo-Drama V: The Last Act, 382

c. Otherness Is Good

Love is found only in distance,
unity only in difference.
Heart of the World, 217

Being distinct from something is the
prerequisite for proximity to it.
*The Glory of the Lord V: The Realm of Metaphysics in the
Modern Age*, 425

Love is not possible without distance, without difference,
without otherness. Without these, there can be no loving
exchange of the gift of self. First and foremost, this is true
within the divine life of God; in order for God's essence to
be love, there must be "otherness" within God:

God's very nature contains otherness:
the Son, who never becomes the Father,
and the Spirit, who never becomes either
the Son or the Father;... this eternal otherness
is the prior condition without which it would
be impossible to call God "love".
Explorations in Theology V: Man Is Created, 65

God the Father grants the Son the "space"
in which he, too, can be the same one God,
while both grant this same "space" to the
Holy Spirit. Being God means making
"room" for the other in oneself.
Explorations in Theology V: Man Is Created, 53

Because love is good, and because otherness makes love
possible, otherness is good, too, a point that was empha-
sized by some of the Scholastic theologians, who formulated

the axiom that "the difference between the One and the
Other in God is something primordially positive."[4] Acting
out of the divine love and freedom, God also makes space
for us human beings, and all of creation, within the space
that exists between the Father and the Son:

> Only such a Trinity is capable of ensheltering
> the whole creation, with all its differences,
> in the space of the difference between the
> Father and the Son who is forsaken by him,
> even as this space is held open by the
> substantial love of both: the Holy Spirit.
> *Explorations in Theology V: Man Is Created*, 415

And because difference/otherness is good within the
divine life, the fact that we are different from, and other
than, God is also good, for it makes love possible between
God and us:

> God, in order to hold to the name love, wills
> to be *in himself* gift and fruitfulness. It is his
> sovereign will to accord space within his unity
> to the "other". Christianity asserts that this
> positive otherness of God justifies the
> being-other of the creature in relation to God.
> *Epilogue*, 35

> For it is a world that has been characterized
> [by God] as "very good" (Gen 1:31) even
> in its very difference from God.
> *Explorations in Theology IV: Spirit and Institution*, 430

---

[4] Hans Urs von Balthasar, *Theo-Logic: Theological Logical Theory*, vol. 2, *Truth of God*, trans. Adrian J. Walker (San Francisco: Ignatius Press, 2004), 82.

The difference between God and us makes it possible for us to enter into a loving union with God while still retaining our identities as unique persons. In our union with God, our individuality is not dissolved, but preserved within the otherness that is integral to the divine life:

> This incorporation of all created beings into the Begotten is, in trinitarian terms, the most intimate manner of union with God. For it implies that the creaturely "other-than-God" is plunged into the uncreated "Other-in-God" *while maintaining* that fundamental "distance" which alone makes love possible.
> *Theo-Drama V: The Last Act*, 105

> How far we now are from the notion that man must negate his I or extinguish it as mere appearance in order to enter into communication with the infinite "I"! Rather, man now knows himself as willed, created and affirmed in his difference. And this consciousness does not leave him orphaned outside God, for he now knows that he has been willed, created and affirmed within the divine differentiation itself. Only in the trinitarian difference can God be in himself the unity of love. And when man enters into this trinitarian difference ("I no longer call you servants but friends"; "We are born of God"), he can participate in the unity of absolute love, which now also includes the love of one's neighbor.
> *Explorations in Theology IV:*
> *Spirit and Institution,* 37

As Balthasar mentions at the end of the last passage, "unity-in-difference" also holds true of love between human beings. Our difference from (i.e., our "non-identity" with) other human beings makes possible the exchange of the gift of self and therefore loving union between human beings:

> Only where there is non-identity is love possible.
> And it is absolutely not true that love requires
> the abolition of personality, that it craves to
> be the Thou of the other. Even in the human
> sphere it wills rather the ever-greater exaltation
> and ecstasy of the beloved *simultaneously* with
> the greatest proximity and communion.
> "The Fathers, the Scholastics, and Ourselves", 355

I would like to close this chapter with a passage that ties together many of the previous reflections regarding the connections between "otherness" and love and adds a reference to the beautiful fruitfulness that the "unity-in-difference" of love makes possible:

> Creation is "the other" over against God. It is
> good that there is this "other", for it is eternally
> good that there is "another" in God; and this
> "other" does not separate but, in the Spirit,
> unites the two and fills them with life. So we
> need not lament the fact that we are not God,
> that we are eternally separated from him by the
> chasm of our creaturely nature; for *because* we
> are "other" than he, we can be his image. More
> than that, we are destined for a union with him
> that is inconceivably profound—deeper than any
> pantheism can imagine—precisely because it

does not obliterate the difference between him
and us. For that same reason the difference
between the creatures themselves, and the fact
that, in all their modes of union, they remain
"themselves", can be held to be "very good";
even in the world of living things the union
of things that are different and distinct brings
forth the mystery of fruitfulness, not only
in the sexual area but in every genuinely
loving encounter in other areas too.

You Crown the Year with Your Goodness, 143

6

Selflessness

a. Being for Oneself vs. Being for Others

In this chapter, we will be reflecting upon what is probably the most difficult element of genuine love for people to live out: selflessness. Balthasar writes at length, and in a variety of ways, about selflessness. In this section, we will focus on the way in which Balthasar frames the selflessness required by love as a choice between "being for oneself" and "being for others". God calls us to choose to "be for others" in love as the three Persons of the Trinity are "for one another" and "for us":

> In God there is absolutely no "for oneself";
> rather, eternal life—absolute life—takes
> place in self-giving for each other.
> *You Have Words of Eternal Life*, 89

> God is never first and foremost for himself:
> from all eternity he is there for the Other.
> *You Crown the Year with Your Goodness*, 159

> This unity [among the three Persons of the
> Trinity] is nothing other than pure being-for-
> one-another. If there were a definition of God,
> then one would have to put it in the form:

unity as being-for-one-another.... One cannot
understand the Father except in his giving of
himself in the begetting of his begotten Son,
nor can one understand the Son except in his
being for the Father. The self-giving of both to
each other is further a "being-for-one-another"
which in the writings of the New Covenant is
clearly distinguished as "Holy Spirit" both from
the Father and from the Son; it is personified
"being-for-one-another" itself and the total
self-giving of God to men.

Elucidations, 92–93

By taking on human flesh and demonstrating how we
are called to be both "for God" and "for neighbor",
Jesus serves as the archetype for us of "being for others".
Balthasar refers to this as Jesus' "being-for",[1] sometimes
abbreviating this to Jesus' "forness".[2] Jesus shows us how
"being for others" frees us from the prison of egoism and
enables us to enter into the divine freedom, which is the
freedom of forness:

[Christ's "forness"] has no other goal than to
free men from the prison of "for self" and to
introduce them to the shape of divine freedom.

You Have Words of Eternal Life, 89

How can we enter into Christ's "forness"? How can we
transcend our egocentrism and choose to live for God

---

[1] Hans Urs von Balthasar, *Theo-Drama: Theological Dramatic Theory*, vol. 4,
The Action, trans. Graham Harrison (San Francisco: Ignatius Press, 1994), 421.

[2] Hans Urs von Balthasar, *You Have Words of Eternal Life: Scripture Meditations*,
trans. Dennis Martin (San Francisco: Ignatius Press, 1991), 89.

and neighbor? Only through God dwelling within us and empowering us to love in such a selfless manner:

> God is the self-giving triune love within
> [the Christian]. It is within this love that
> each person exists solely for the other and
> knows nothing of "being-for-oneself".
> *Light of the Word*, 46–47

Although such a radical renunciation of self-interest can be extremely difficult (even with God's help), the results of transcending one's selfish desires will be far more reward-ing than what Balthasar correctly calls the "boredom" of remaining enclosed within one's own ego:

> In God being a person means surrender, love, and
> fruitfulness, and only in that way is God eternal
> life: as something which holds sway eternally in
> the process of giving of itself and being given
> to, of making blissful and being made blissful.
> The pure opposite of the boredom of an exitless
> being-for-oneself. No, essentially a being-above-
> and-beyond-oneself, with all the surprises and
> adventures that such an excursion promises.
> *Credo*, 101–2

By using our God-given freedom to choose "being for oth-ers" over "being for ourselves", we can break out of the finitude of our egos and begin to enter into the "fullness", the infinite space and freedom of the divine life of God:

> By bursting his boundaries in "being for", [man]
> gains a share in the fullness of divine and cosmic

being, being that comes from the center of the
One who is at once both God and man.
You Have Words of Eternal Life, 90

The more completely we enter into God's form of being-
for-one-another, the more completely God can use our
lives to benefit others:

> Being-for-one-another ... opens up the individual
> to the other precisely from the apex of his
> personality. And this still occurs with increasing
> intensity, the more deeply the believing person
> allows himself to be determined, to be taken up
> into and, as it were, dispossessed by this divine
> form of being-for-one-another. Whoever gives
> his consent to this divine form of life, to a life in
> which from the outset one abandons all claim to
> possession in favor of the other, whoever holds
> out for the other's disposal everything which
> belongs to him, including that which is most
> private and apparently most incommunicable, of
> such a man the God of love disposes in all truth
> and effectiveness for the benefit of his brothers.
> *Elucidations*, 94

Renouncing self-interest in order to love God and neighbor in this life prepares us for the divine life of being-for-
one-another into which we will enter more fully in the
life to come:

> The state of "existing for oneself" here below,
> conditioned by mortality, [will give] way in

heaven to the truly personal, trinitarian
"existing for others, away from oneself".
Life Out of Death, 86

b. *Ekstasis*

The phrase found at the end of the previous section,
"existing for others, *away from oneself*", enables us to
make a connection between the choice to "be for" others
and another aspect of the selflessness required by genuine love, an aspect that Balthasar sometimes refers to as
"*ekstasis*". *Ekstasis* is a Greek word that literally means "to
stand outside of oneself".[3] To "be for others", one has
to be willing to break out of the self-enclosure of one's
egocentrism and move outward in openness toward the
Other (God) and others (our "neighbor", i.e., *all* human
beings) in order to receive and give the gift of self. One
must "stand outside of oneself", finding one's center
(and, thereby, finding one's true self) in the Other and
others rather than in the finitude of one's own being.[4]

In a particularly revealing etymological connection,
our English word "ecstasy", whose meaning includes "an
overwhelming feeling of great happiness or joyful excite-
ment",[5] is derived from the Greek term *ekstasis*. As we will
see in the chapter on the intimate connection between
love and happiness (chapter 12), our greatest happiness lies
in this movement of love out of oneself and into the Other

[3] *The New Oxford American Dictionary*, 2nd ed. (Oxford: Oxford University
Press, 2005), s.v. "ecstasy".

[4] For further discussion of this concept of *ekstasis*, see Benedict XVI, Encyc-
lical Letter *God Is Love: Deus Caritas Est* (San Francisco: Ignatius Press, 2006),
no. 6.

[5] *The New Oxford American Dictionary*, 2nd ed., s.v. "ecstasy".

who is God and the others who are our neighbors. True *ecstasy* is found in the *ekstasis* of love.

By now, the reader will not be surprised to learn that the *ekstasis* to which we are called is found first and foremost within the life of the Trinity (also, please notice the connection to *Hingabe*, or self-surrender):

> Just as the Divine Persons are *themselves* only
> insofar as they go out to the Others (who
> are always Other), the created essences too
> are *themselves* only insofar as they go beyond
> themselves and indicate their primal ground
> (whence being in its totality shines forth) and
> their vocation of self-surrender. They are
> to surrender themselves for their neighbor
> (whoever he may be); thus, concretely,
> they offer their self-surrender through every
> particular instance to Being in its totality.
> *Theo-Drama V: The Last Act*, 76

In the following passage, Balthasar claims that all created beings are stamped with the *ekstasis* of the Creator, in that all created being is marked by a movement "from its interior to the exterior", i.e., by a movement from self-enclosure to the self-disclosure and self-gift that are the basis of "the good, the true, and the beautiful" (we will look more specifically at the connection between love and these three "transcendental" aspects of being in chapters 15–17).

> Every created being is a manifestation of itself
> (the more intensively the higher it ranks): the
> representation of its own depths, the surface
> of its own ground, the word from its essential

core; and upon this essential movement of being
(from its interior to the exterior) are founded
the good, the true, and the beautiful.
The Glory of the Lord I: Seeing the Form, 593

In this regard, Balthasar affirms a point made by Denys
the Areopagite over 1,500 years ago: that being itself is
"ecstatic towards God" in imitation of the divine movement of love toward the world.

Certainly it is true that according to Denys the
essence of each being is itself ecstatic towards
God (something that so little threatens its
individuality that this movement itself determines
it at its deepest level); indeed, that this ecstasy of
creaturely *eros* is itself an imitation of the ecstatic
divine *eros* which out of love goes out of itself
into the multiplicity of the world.
The Glory of the Lord II: Studies in Theological Style:
Clerical Styles, 205

Ekstasis is an integral part of the divine life and makes possible the *ekstasis* of God toward the world in the Incarnation of Jesus Christ:

The exteriorisation of God (in the Incarnation)
has its ontic condition of possibility in the
eternal exteriorisation of God—that is,
in his tripersonal self-gift.
Mysterium Paschale, 28

God has ventured outward (so to speak) toward us in
love, and he invites us to respond in a reciprocally ecstatic

movement of love, even *demands* it in the sense that it is in the eternal circulation of love that our ultimate happiness lies. God's "demands" or "commandments" are designed to steer us toward that love in which we will find our ultimate happiness, the happiness for which we were created.

Only via *ekstasis* can we respond appropriately to God's own *ekstasis* toward us in Jesus:

> The *ekstasis* of love, its going out of itself: only
> this way can man achieve an act of serious
> love which corresponds to God's own act of
> taking love seriously—the act of the divine
> Eros which goes out of itself in order to become
> man and die on the Cross for the world.[6]
> *The Glory of the Lord I: Seeing the Form*, 210

> Each of us who has the Spirit must live outside
> himself, in love to the other, in the other.
> *Light of the Word*, 273

Balthasar, who places tremendous emphasis on the necessity of prayer and contemplation for the life of the Christian, notes that contemplation can "catapult" us out of our self-enclosed life and into the ultimate fulfillment of self that is to be found by participating in the divine *ekstasis* of love:

> In becoming aware of the extent of the divine
> self-giving, the individual who meditates is
> catapulted out of his would-be closed personal

---

[6] Balthasar bases this passage, in part, on Denys the Areopagite, *De divinis nominibus*, IV, 13.

being, not into a destruction of his personhood
but into its fulfillment: the creature's attainable
approximation to the unalloyed being-for-others
within the divine, trinitarian mystery.
Christian Meditation, 84

It is in the Thou, then, that we find our I.
Convergences, 128

If I stay locked within myself, if I seek myself,
I shall not find the peace that is promised to
the man on whom God's favor rests. I must
go. I must enter the service of the poor and
imprisoned. I must lose my soul if I am to regain
it, for so long as I hold onto it, I shall lose it.
You Crown the Year with Your Goodness, 278

The paths of love that we are intended to tread force us
out of the familiarity and comfort of our self-enclosed egos
and into the "wilderness" of love:

Every road pushes me violently out
of myself and into the wilderness.
Heart of the World, 214

We must venture out of ourselves into the "wilderness of
love" if we are to participate in the eternal circulation
of love and life within the Body of Christ:

Nothing bears fruit without being pierced
open—an organism with inward circulation
closed in upon itself accomplishes nothing;
rather, life must make its way outside, and it
flows best out of the center that keeps life

circulating. How else could the mystical
body of Christ come into being?[7]

You Have Words of Eternal Life, 61

c. Kenosis

The necessary meaning of being is manifested in
being's self-emptying as the gift of love.

Theo-Logic III: The Spirit of Truth, 228

In addition to *ekstasis*, Balthasar uses a second Greek term
in discussing the selflessness of love: *kenosis. Kenosis* literally means "emptying",[8] but is used by Balthasar in the
more specific sense of *self*-emptying. Relying in part on
the kenotic theology of the Russian Orthodox theologian
Sergei Bulgakov, Balthasar describes the way in which the
three Persons of the Trinitarian God "empty themselves"
out in order to give and receive the total gift of self to and
from each other, beginning with God the Father:

It is possible to say, with Bulgakov, that the
Father's self-utterance in the generation of the
Son is an initial "kenosis" within the Godhead
that underpins all subsequent kenosis. For the
Father strips himself, without remainder, of
his Godhead and hands it over to the Son; he
"imparts" to the Son all that is his. "All that is
thine is mine" (Jn 17:10). The Father ... *is* this
movement of self-giving that holds nothing back.

Theo-Drama IV: The Action, 323

[7] Please note the eloquent connection between openness and *ekstasis* drawn
by Balthasar in this passage.

[8] *The New Oxford American Dictionary*, 2nd ed., s.v. "kenosis".

The initial kenosis of God the Father in begetting God the Son expands to the entire Trinity in the reciprocal self-emptying of the Son and of the Holy Spirit. These intra-Trinitarian kenoses make possible the kenotic movements of God toward the world, including bestowing freedom upon human beings in the creation of the world, entering into a sacred covenant with the Israelites, and taking on human nature in the Incarnation of God the Son:

> We spoke of a first "kenosis" of the Father,
> expropriating himself by "generating" the
> consubstantial Son. Almost automatically, this
> first kenosis expands to a kenosis involving
> the whole Trinity. For the Son could not be
> consubstantial with the Father except by self-expropriation; and their "We", that is, the
> Spirit, must also be God if he is to be the
> "personal" seal of that self-expropriation that
> is identical in Father and Son. For the Spirit
> does not want anything "for himself" but,
> as his revelation in the world shows, wants
> simply to be the pure manifestation and
> communication of the love between Father and
> Son (Jn 14:26; 16:13–15). This primal kenosis
> makes possible all other kenotic movements
> of God into the world; they are simply its
> consequences. The first "self-limitation" of the
> triune God arises through endowing his creatures
> with freedom. The second, deeper, "limitation"
> of the same triune God occurs as a result of the
> covenant, which, on God's side, is indissoluble,
> whatever may become of Israel. The third
> kenosis, which is not only christological but

involves the whole Trinity, arises through
the Incarnation of the Son alone.

Theo-Drama IV: The Action, 331

Christ, as the Father's Word sent and incarnate,
passes over from the *forma Dei* [form of God]
in which he abides into the *forma Servi*
[form of a servant].

Explorations in Theology II: Spouse of the Word, 137

[In the piercing of Jesus' heart on the Cross]
the place of [Jesus'] heart is open, empty,
for all to enter; in this self-emptying, the
kenosis has reached its fulfillment.

The Glory of the Lord VII: Theology:
The New Covenant, 226

The [Holy] Spirit's perfect freedom to blow
whither he will, to distribute gifts as he will, arises
from the renunciation of both Father and Son:
both refuse to be understood except in terms
of self-emptying. Their bestowal of freedom
presupposes this self-emptying, this *kenosis.*

Theo-Logic III: The Spirit of Truth, 241

[The Holy Spirit] gives place to Father and
Son in a kind of *kenosis* (which is why he
is so hard to grasp as a Person).

Theo-Logic III: The Spirit of Truth, 147

In discussing the kenotic aspects of self-giving love within
the Trinity, Balthasar makes repeated use of the themes of
"poverty" and "wealth". He does so in order to express
the profound spiritual paradox that the greatest wealth,
true wealth, is found only by first making oneself "poor":

by emptying oneself in order to enter *completely* into the receptivity and donativity of self-giving love. In fact, *everything* that is good and that we human beings most deeply desire (happiness, meaning, freedom, peace, "wealth", "power", etc.) is ultimately found by using our God-given freedom to accept God's invitation to join in the divine life of self-giving love.

Here are a few of the passages in which Balthasar highlights the identity of wealth and poverty within the kenoses of the intra-Trinitarian life and in God's extension of that life to us via creation and the Incarnation, death, and Resurrection of Jesus:

> The divine Father is Father from all eternity.
> That means that his generation of the Son
> is always prior; from before all time the Father
> has given all that he has to his Son; he has
> never possessed anything by himself that
> he had not already, from all eternity, given
> away. In fact, this giving away constitutes his
> most distinctive, divine wealth. God is the
> richest of all because he is the poorest of all.
> *You Crown the Year with Your Goodness*, 230

> It is clear from the words of Jesus about
> his relationship with the Father that they
> interpenetrate in their reciprocal loving self-
> surrender. Both renounce being a mere "I"
> without a "thou": this allows us to glimpse the
> identity of poverty and wealth in the divine love;
> for wealth and fullness are found in the self-
> surrendering Other (this also applies to the Father,
> since without the Son he could

not be Father). Since this wealth—with its
implicit renunciation—is experienced by
both as a single gift, and neither keeps account
of the renunciation it demanded, the wealth
of both (which in each case is a *received*
wealth) coincides in a oneness.
Theo-Logic III: The Spirit of Truth, 226

God's entire wealth consists in this giving
of self and receiving of the "Thou".
You Crown the Year with Your Goodness, 231

What we have here [in the self-emptying
and self-giving of the Father, Son, and Holy
Spirit] is the identity of "having" and
"giving", of wealth and poverty.
Theo-Drama II: The Dramatis Personae:
Man in God, 256–57

The power of love ... transcends the antithesis
between poverty and wealth (it is both at once).
Theo-Logic II: Truth of God, 141

[The divine] nature is always both what is
possessed and what is given away, and we
cannot say that a particular hypostasis is
rich in possessing and poor in giving away,
for the fullness of blessedness [i.e., bliss,
happiness] lies in both giving and receiving
both the gift and the giver.
Theo-Drama II: The Dramatis Personae:
Man in God, 258

Love cannot store up anything for itself. It
consists, in fact, in the opposite movement,

not storing up but giving away. And the more
it gives away and becomes poor, the richer it
becomes toward God. Why? Because God himself
is Love, pure and simple, and his entire wealth
consists in self-giving and self-emptying. . . .
Certainly the Christian God, as the revelation
of Jesus Christ shows him to us, is almighty, and
so he is infinitely rich. But what form does his
infinite wealth take? God the Father, the origin
of everything, gives away himself and all that
he is and has to his only-begotten Son, who in
turn does not store up all this treasure within
himself but acknowledges it as the Father's gift
and returns it to him; these Two by no means
stay enclosed in a kind of mutual egoism but,
in mutual selflessness, cause the Holy Spirit to
proceed from them, the Spirit of absolute love,
the epitome of eternal wealth in this unceasing
exchange of gifts. Even though *God's triune nature*
remains a profound mystery, we can grasp this: in
God, wealth and power are not qualities existing
side by side with love and external to it; they are
identical with it. God only *has* insofar as he *gives*,
and this giving is of his innermost essence. . . . God
is never first and foremost for himself: from all
eternity he is there for the Other. God only exists
as Father in his eternal act of self-surrender to
the Son. This is his whole wealth, his whole
power. We cannot imagine it, and yet it is so: in
God, self-emptying and self-impoverishment
coincide with self-being and richness.
        You Crown the Year with Your Goodness, 158–59

God's endless wealth is found in his self-giving
and self-emptying, that is, in the very
opposite of the wish to have everything.
Light of the Word, 336

[Jesus'] "having" a human nature, which is given
away without reserve in the Eucharist, is therefore
nothing other than the earthly representation of
the trinitarian poverty, in which everything
is always already given away.
Theo-Drama V: The Last Act, 516

Human beings were created in the image of the "self-
emptying God", and our ultimate fulfillment lies in imitating God's kenotic love:

In his "kenosis" God shows man that, right from
the outset, he (man) is constructed according
to a kenotic principle. It is precisely in this
self-emptying and poverty that he will become—
and already is—rich and glorious.
In the Fullness of Faith, 115

Going out of ourselves and into "the other"
is a sign both of poverty and of wealth.
Theo-Drama II: The Dramatis Personae: Man in God, 228

Our wealth is this: to receive this self-giving
[of Jesus] and to respond to it by handing
it on. A process of love.
You Crown the Year with Your Goodness, 293

In Christ's Church, one possesses only in
order to give and is enriched that way.
Life Out of Death, 87

God initiates this movement toward kenotic love within us at Baptism by "unselving" us to make room for Jesus Christ within our hearts. Baptism is the first step in what is to become a lifelong process of increasingly deepening our imitation of the admittedly inimitable divine kenosis:

Being thus dead and risen to new life [by being baptized into Christ] is not an external attribute of our self, however: death and resurrection *change* it. [The self] is not annihilated in a Buddhist sense but *unselved* by being drawn into the death and life of Christ. It is forced out of its central position so that the essence of Christ may take up residence there: "I have been crucified with Christ; it is no longer I who live, but Christ who lives in me; and the life I now live in the flesh I live by faith in the Son of God, who loved me and gave himself for me" (Gal 2:20). The same abandonment of self is required of all who believe in Christ: "None of us lives to himself, and none of us dies to himself. If we live, we live to the Lord, and if we die, we die to the Lord; so then, whether we live or whether we die, we are the Lord's" (Rom 14:7–8; cf. the Lord's abandonment of self in Rom 6:10–11). Faith's effect of "unselving" us creates a "vacant space" that is occupied by Christ and his "Spirit", who "confirms" to us that we, like the Son, are children of the Father, sharing a relation to the Son through the Spirit, so that the *imago trinitatis* [image of the Trinity] is fulfilled in us.

Theo-Drama V: The Last Act, 334

The *kenosis* ... of Christ cannot be imitated, but a
possible configuration to [it] lies in making oneself
empty of oneself (cf. Matt 5.8) in order to be
filled by the active "image" of the love of God
in Christ which imprints itself on one.

The Glory of the Lord VII: Theology: New Covenant, 294

God gave us everything in Christ, and therefore we must
empty ourselves to make room for Christ and the Holy
Spirit:

In Christ God gives man everything; hence the
requirement to set aside all of one's own in
order to make room for this "one and all".

Light of the Word, 104

The more pliable, abandoned, and free from
his self-form the believer is, the better can
the divine image and the form of Christ
be impressed on him.

Explorations in Theology II: Spouse of the Word, 107

As *Holy* Spirit he can enter only someone who
is "poor in spirit" (Mt 5:3), that is, someone
who has emptied and opened up his own spirit
to make room for the Spirit of God.

Light of the Word, 85

This act of making room itself has a profoundly
eucharistic character. Kenosis is an emptying
out to provide a space that can be filled.

New Elucidations, 126

God needs selfless vessels into which he
can pour his essential selflessness.

New Elucidations, 44

> [Jesus speaking to each of us:] Empty
> yourself out into me so completely
> that I can fill you with myself.
> *Heart of the World*, 199

In the following passage, Balthasar makes some specific references to what we may have to empty ourselves of in order to make more room for God within us, and he asserts that such self-emptying is identical to faith:

> Leaving all things means a spiritual renunciation
> of one's own views, mode of life, and purposes
> and, on a deeper level, of one's own freedom
> and reason, offering them all to the Master, and,
> according to his disposition, either receiving them
> back or not, or having them replaced by his
> own purposes and freedom and reason. In this,
> leaving all things is the same thing as *faith*.
> *Explorations in Theology II: Spouse of the Word*, 97

We are to empty ourselves not only to make more room for God in our hearts, but also to make more room for other people, in the receptive openness required by genuine love:

> To live with another within the compass
> of one heart: I must move to the side,
> must make myself small, so that the other
> has space and does not feel crowded.
> *The Grain of Wheat*, 9

We are also called to empty ourselves in order to make it more possible for us to give the gift of self to both God and neighbor, in the donative openness required by genuine love:

Interior self-renunciation (*Entselbstung*,
literally "unselving") has not only its effect,
but its basis and constant verification in self-
renunciation for the purpose of serving the
world—serving the historical Christ, whom I
encounter through the Church and in her, and,
if I have understood the Gospel, also in every
neighbour and in every situation in the world.

The Glory of the Lord I: Seeing the Form, 210

d. Love Is Tested through Sacrifice

Earlier (in chapter 6a), I claimed that selflessness is probably the most difficult element of love for people to live
out. In this section and the next, we will focus upon the
aspects of selflessness that many people find to be the most
challenging: making sacrifices and enduring suffering, perhaps even death, out of love.

Although the present section focuses specifically on the
role that sacrifice plays in love, the motif of sacrifice has actually been woven, either explicitly or implicitly, throughout
all of the chapters of part 2 of this book. To surrender oneself to others in love; to "pour oneself out" in the gift of
self; to enter deeply into the movements of receptivity and
donativity; to open oneself to love and thus to the vulnera-
bility and the pain that love can bring; to choose to "be for
others" rather than to "be for oneself"; to venture out of
the familiar confines of one's ego and into the infinite spaces
of love; to empty oneself of the egocentric concerns and
preoccupations that can get in the way of love: clearly, all of
these require *sacrifice*. For Balthasar, sacrifice is an indispens-
able component of genuine love; indeed, the genuineness

of love is tested by its willingness to sacrifice for the sake of
the beloved:

> Love makes us free if it is selfless, and it is selfless
> if it is ready to sacrifice pleasure, advantage and
> independence for the sake of the beloved. And
> since no earthly love is initially perfect, it must go
> through these purifications. Moments and times
> must come when love is tested through sacrifice,
> when it becomes clear whether the enthusiasm of
> the first encounter was love at all, when the naïve
> first love—if it really was love—is refined and
> deepened in the fire of renunciation.
>
> *Prayer,* 128

> Love is always ready to renounce what
> is its own for the sake of others.
>
> *Theo-Logic I: Truth of the World,* 130

If we are honest with ourselves, we will acknowledge that
genuine love requires sacrifice, but we often seek the joy of
love without being willing to make the requisite sacrifices:

> [Man] recognizes a moral imperative, not just as
> an indifferent law to which he is subject, but as
> that which will lead him to his true freedom. But
> he also feels an unwillingness to follow this lead,
> a laziness that weighs him down, a sluggishness
> of the heart that would rather abide by itself than
> embark on the strenuousness of love. Love means
> self-conquest, and so even as a child one seeks a
> way of having the pleasure of love without self-
> conquest. He wants to win the affection of the

world without exerting the self; this is the essence
of nonlove disguised as love; this is lust.
A Theological Anthropology, 50

Spiritual joy cannot be gained without
the pain of renunciation.
Truth Is Symphonic, 124

There are the family joys: They are purchased
with countless sacrifices and renunciations.
Convergences, 112

All who deny themselves in order to carry out
love's commission are on the right path.
You Crown the Year with Your Goodness, 280

Genuine love requires sacrificial *deeds*, not just words:

It is easy to say "I love you". We need to prove
it. The deeds that demonstrate our words are
always bodily deeds. We do something for the
beloved person; we take pains, go out of our way,
give up some of our time.... In interpersonal
love too, therefore, the word must become
flesh in order to manifest its truth.
You Crown the Year with Your Goodness, 148

Speech between human beings is not ultimate:
beyond it is the proof of the deed.
Theo-Logic II: Truth of God, 120

God, whose very essence is love, is not merely some
abstract idea of love, but *active* love, as is shown by the
sacrificial self-giving found within the life of the Trinity
and in Jesus Christ's self-sacrifice on behalf of the world:

God ... has shown himself to be pure, free,
absolute love: not an "idea of love", but
love itself, concrete and active.
Explorations in Theology V: Man Is Created, 32

There is a certain quality of "renunciation" in
the eternal trinitarian life: it is seen in the very
fact that "the Father, renouncing his uniqueness,
generates the Son out of his own substance."[9]
Theo-Drama V: The Last Act, 510

[Jesus] proclaims himself to be the divine
Father's Word to the world and proves this
claim through his complete obedience to God
and his total self-surrender to and for the world.
Love ... is only proved by deeds of flesh and
blood. Here the deed consists in the body
of Jesus being broken as he suffers for all the
world's sin and in his blood being poured out
for all the world's self-asserting egoists.
You Crown the Year with Your Goodness, 150

We are called to share in Jesus Christ's sacrifice for others,
in fact, for the whole world. Balthasar has referred to this
as our being "co-sacrificed" with Christ.[10]

In [Romans 12:1–2] Paul summarizes in simple
words the lifelong task of Christians: in light of
God's mercy they should offer themselves bodily

[9] Balthasar is quoting Adrienne von Speyr (*I Korinther*, 345), in obvious
agreement with her.
[10] Hans Urs von Balthasar, *A Short Primer for Unsettled Laymen*, trans. Sister
Mary Theresilde Skerry (San Francisco: Ignatius Press, 1985), 108.

as a living and holy sacrifice, which constitutes
true worship suited to Christ the Word....
Christian existence, if lived according to the
Logos—in imitation of Christ, is thereby
both a sermon to the world and a sacrifice for
the world, since Christians have their share
in Christ's self-sacrifice for the world.

Light of the Word, 123–24

Your salvation does not consist in
eliminating your "I" but in sacrificing
your "I" for others, which cannot take
place without pain and the cross.

Light of the Word, 122

We were created to share in the joy of love, which also
means that we were made to participate in the sacrifices
that are an essential component of love:

Our existence, in its very foundations,
is structured for sacrifice.

The Grain of Wheat, 34

e. Fluid in the Flowing Spirit

Suffering, like sacrifice, is one of the ways that love can
prove its genuineness (of course, sacrifice and suffering are
often intertwined, in that sacrifice often involves suffering). In fact, Balthasar asserts that suffering on behalf of
another person, perhaps even to the point of dying for the
sake of that other person, expresses the ultimacy of one's
love like no other expression of love could. When this is
understood, both the lover and the beloved can rejoice in

that suffering, not because they value suffering for suffering's sake, but because the suffering is undergone out of
love and is therefore profoundly meaningful and beautiful.
The following passage from Balthasar is referring in particular to Jesus ("the beloved") suffering and dying on behalf
of his disciples out of love for his disciples, but it is clear
that Balthasar also intends to express a general truth about
suffering that is undergone out of love for others:

> It is the lover who rejoices that the beloved
> suffers: not because suffering would be a joy, but
> because suffering is an expression of his love,
> which could not have expressed its ultimacy in
> any other way ([Jn] 15.13). The beloved rejoices
> that he is permitted to do this, and therefore
> the lover too should rejoice in this.
>
> *The Glory of the Lord VII: Theology:*
> *The New Covenant,* 538–39

Balthasar would undoubtedly agree with a similar statement made by Adrienne von Speyr, the Catholic convert
and mystic for whom Balthasar served as spiritual director:
"The suffering on the Cross is the expression of the love
within God. The expression chosen by God to show us
the mystery of his love; in order to be able to reveal itself,
love suffers."[11]

If we reflect on these statements, they ring true. Is there
any more definitive way to show one's love for another
than to be willing to suffer, even to die, on that person's
behalf? This is why Balthasar asserts that genuine love is

---

[11] Adrienne von Speyr, "The Fire of God Is a Suffering", in Hans Urs von
Balthasar and Adrienne von Speyr, *To the Heart of the Mystery of Redemption,*
trans. Anne Englund Nash (San Francisco: Ignatius Press, 2010), 73.

"a love that wants to suffer".[12] This is referring, not to a masochistic love, a love that derives pleasure from suffering itself, but rather to the depth of a love that is *willing* to suffer, out of love, for the sake of another person.

Balthasar has much more to say about the connections that can exist between love and suffering. In several passages, he points out how suffering can serve an "educative function":

> The Greek play on words *pathei manthanein*, to
> learn by suffering, proves true in everyone.
> *New Elucidations*, 260

> Only through the experience of suffering
> does man acquire true knowledge
> of God and of himself.
> *The Glory of the Lord I: Seeing the Form*, 256

> Suffering has an educative function, makes
> us aware of the seriousness of life and
> death and of man's final goal.
> *Theo-Drama IV: The Action*, 192

The witnessing of suffering or, what is often even more powerful, the personal *experience* of suffering can raise existential issues that set us on the path to discovering self-giving love as the ultimate reality. One of the first steps toward such a realization can be brought about when an experience of suffering jars us out of our "ensconcement" in the comforts of a self-serving life, ensconcement in the familiarity and seeming security of one's self-enclosed ego:

---

[12] Hans Urs von Balthasar, *Heart of the World*, trans. Erasmo S. Leiva (San Francisco: Ignatius Press, 1979), 80.

Some particular suffering—temporary or chronic,
bodily or mental—can itself be meaningful,
even beneficial, for his overall spiritual health
as a person. It might be just the stimulant he
needs to preserve him from the imperceptible
process of spiritual decay brought on by
ensconcement in bourgeois comfort.
Explorations in Theology V: Man Is Created, 105

At a practical level, witnessing suffering in others can moti-
vate people to take action to alleviate suffering:

Suffering spurs man on to fight against it;
this is most definitely part of his task in
the world, stimulating him to make countless
discoveries.... [S]uffering prompts countless
people to engage in acts of love of neighbor....
People must go hungry so that others may
have compassion and selflessly give them bread.
People must be sick or in prison so that others
may hit upon the idea of visiting them.... In
the drama between heaven and earth, therefore,
human suffering is in many ways an element
contributing to the gravity of the action.
Theo-Drama IV: The Action, 192

Thus, suffering, whether we experience it ourselves or
witness it in others, can spur us to break out of our egoism and steer us onto the path of love. Suffering can help
to educate us in the selflessness of genuine love. As such,
suffering is pretty much a required course in the school of
love that is this earthly life:

Are we sure that the difficult, painful, insufferable, absolutely unendurable thing might not be precisely the way in which God's love wants to lead us—into a depth and refinement that we could never have reached without suffering?

You Have Words of Eternal Life, 186

The divine fire needs fuel that it can transform, purify and transfigure into effulgent bodies. Whether sinful or not, the finite must somehow or other die into God, surrender its "for-itself" in order to live in the only ultimate "in-itself"; and this transition—ecstasy, burning, death— will be pain, or at least something analogous to pain. Accordingly, we read in the writings of all the mystics that *God's fire wounds by healing and heals by wounding*, that, in this regard, being wounded and being healed are one and the same thing, that ascent into heaven is unthinkable without descent into hell.

New Elucidations, 277–78

There can be no properly Christian conversion without a piercing of the heart, because only the man whose heart is pierced loves, and only the man who loves—the man whose spiritual substance truly flows out of him—can be called "healthy" in a fully Christian sense. There is no true health of the soul besides authentic, self-giving love.

Explorations in Theology V: Man Is Created, 284

Does there not have to be an opening, a wound, a painful hurt, so that something of my self can

flow out of me as a balm to heal others and make
them whole? Woe to those who make their way
through life like closed, windowless monads,
existentially blind to the inner lives of others....
It is only when my best substance flows out of me
that God can strengthen others through me.
Explorations in Theology V: Man Is Created, 283–84

And if we are given to suffer, deeper shafts are
sunk in us than we thought we could contain,
depths destined to become, in the life everlasting,
reservoirs of greater happiness, wells still more
productive. Wells that flow forth of themselves,
gratis; for in the life everlasting, all is gratis.
Credo, 103

Suffering in this world does not lead us away
from God but toward God, a confirmation
that grows into certainty through the Spirit of
the love of God that is poured out in our hearts.
Suffering makes us more fluid in the flowing
Spirit, makes us flow into the eternally
circulating stream of divine love.
Light of the Word, 312

Balthasar's statement that "suffering makes us more fluid
in the flowing Spirit, makes us flow into the eternally circulating stream of divine love", contains a deep insight
into the potential connection between the experience of
suffering and growth in our ability to love and, therefore,
into the potential value and meaningfulness of suffering
itself. We live in a society that generally seeks to avoid
suffering at all costs, but suffering can play a key role in
breaking down the self-protective wall we build around

our egos, helping to soften our hearts and open them up
more fully to love.

Perhaps the most profound way in which suffering can
enable us to "flow into the eternally circulating stream of
divine love" is when we freely choose to accept our suffering (and even our eventual death) in a spirit of love and
to unite it with the suffering and death that Jesus Christ
underwent out of love for all human beings. Doing so
enables us to participate in Jesus' redemptive love for the
whole world:

> I think that the proclamation of the Cross can
> help men accept sufferings that often seem
> intolerable, to accept them, not because a God
> suffers in solidarity with them—how would that
> relieve them?—but because a divine suffering
> encompasses all these sufferings in order to
> transform them into prayer, into a dialogue in
> the midst of abandonment, thereby conferring
> on all human tragedies a meaning they would
> not have in themselves, a meaning that is in the
> end redemptive for the salvation of the world; all
> suffering being taken up secretly, mysteriously,
> into the sacrifice of the crucified Christ: of the
> Head who is inseparable from his members.
>
> *To the Heart of the Mystery of Redemption*, 39

> Christ's mission on our behalf is more than a
> work and a suffering on his part to spare others
> the punishment they have justly deserved ...;
> it involves his coworking and cosuffering with
> those who are estranged from God. In this way,
> the Second Adam [Jesus] opens up an area of

Christian mission in which the latter, *en Christōi*
[in Christ], can be given a share in his salvific
work and suffering for the world.

Theo-Drama III: The Dramatis Personae:
The Person in Christ, 241

The sufferings of the God–man are all-
sufficient, but within those sufferings a
place has been left for [us] disciples.

Theo-Drama IV: The Action, 388

And if it is true that the suffering of the
Crucified One can transform even worldly
pain, unintelligible to itself, into a
co-redemptive suffering, then the most
unbelievable, most cruel tortures, prisons,
concentration camps and whatever other horrors
there may be can be seen in close proximity
to the Cross, to that utter night, interrupted
only by the unfathomable cry of "Why?"

Theo-Drama V: The Last Act, 501

Readiness to accept punishment for our
guilt is inseparable from suffering with Jesus
for all guilt and, therefore, implies readiness
to atone with him for the guilt of others,
both known and unknown.

Christian Meditation, 37

Most of us can understand that suffering *directly* on behalf
of another, or dying in another's place (for example, Saint
Maximillian Kolbe offering himself to be executed by Nazi
concentration camp officers in place of a fellow prisoner
who pleaded not to be killed because he had a wife and

children) can be a profound expression of love, but how can we possibly suffer out of love on behalf of others who are *unknown* to us? The answer to that question can be found in a discussion of the *communio sanctorum* or "communion of saints", which Balthasar has referred to as "the most profound of the Catholic mysteries".[13]

f. *Communio Sanctorum*

[The communion of saints] is a
communion of open hearts.
You Crown the Year with Your Goodness, 224

The "communion of saints" refers to the mysterious connection that exists among all human beings via the redemptive work of Jesus Christ. Whenever any of us engages in a loving action (for example, charitable acts such as feeding the hungry, sheltering the homeless, praying on behalf of others, making sacrifices out of love for others, undergoing suffering or even death on behalf of another, etc.), that action generates spiritual "merits" that God can distribute, as God sees fit, to others who are in need. The most common metaphor that Balthasar uses for the communion of saints is the circulation of "blood" or "fruit" or "spiritual goods" among the members of the Body of Christ:

We have a glimpse into the unfathomable
Mystery that, because Jesus "died for all", no one
may any longer live and die for self alone (2 Cor
5:14f.); but that, in loving selflessness, as much of

---

[13] Hans Urs von Balthasar, *Truth Is Symphonic: Aspects of Christian Pluralism*, trans. Graham Harrison (San Francisco: Ignatius Press, 1987), 63.

the good as anyone possesses belongs to all,
which gives rise to an unending exchange
and circulation of blood between all the
members of the ecclesiastical Body of Christ.
And precisely those members who are designated,
in an eminent sense, as "holy" are like open
treasure-houses accessible to all, like flowing
fountains at which everyone can drink.
Credo, 85

If a mission [of love] is accepted and carried out,
it de-privatizes the "I", causing the latter's fruitful
influence (through grace) to expand into the
whole "Mystical Body" of Christ. In this way,
there is a mutual interpenetration of the diverse
missions and the persons who identify themselves
with them: this is what is meant by the *communio
sanctorum*. Evidently it is not only the goods and
values of these persons that become common
property but the persons themselves.
*Theo-Drama III: The Dramatis Personae:
The Person in Christ*, 349

The mysteries of the communion of the saints
are as unfathomable as that of the Eucharist.
Everyone belonging to it possesses only in
order to give and receives only by giving.
Personality and communion grow with
each other and permeate each other.
Life Out of Death, 87

Not only can people do things externally on
behalf of one another, one person taking a
burden from someone else; now it becomes

possible internally as well: in Christ's Eucharist
a person can share in bearing someone else's
guilt or handicap. The *communio eucharistica*
becomes ... the *communio sanctorum*. And the
form of exchange in the latter is entirely marked
by that of the former and inherent in it.
Theo-Drama II: The Dramatis Personae: Man in God, 410

When we believe that we can call on the saints
at any time and in any place (for example,
the final petition of the Hail Mary), we are
presupposing that the saints have this same
eucharistic openness toward us. This
eucharistic "permeability" of all subjects to
one another, even now in our mortal existence,
is the very basis of the *communio sanctorum*.
Theo-Drama V: The Last Act, 383

The biblical metaphor of the vine (Jesus Christ being the
vine, and the members of his Body being the branches of
that vine; Jn 15:1–17) is also used to describe the communion of saints:

"Through grace", a fellowship of suffering and
resurrection is created, and this fellowship only
has meaning if the *pro nobis* [Jesus Christ suffering
and dying "*for us*" or "*in our place*"] is extended to
the participants. The metaphor of the vine brings
us as close as we can get to uttering its meaning:
the man who lives *en Christōi* [in Christ], from
the root and stem of Christ, will bear fruit....
But this bearing of fruit is not for oneself: it is for
the kingdom of God.... So, however hidden and

modest their contribution is, they are working
within Christ's sphere and in fellowship with him.
Theo-Drama IV: The Action, 388

In the communion of saints the spheres of the
loving parties interpenetrate: each lives from
the others and shares his own with them.
Together they form the Lord's vine. No one
thinks of enriching himself through sharing
with the others; no one calculates how much
he is giving the others. They all think solely
of the Lord's great task in which they share,
the kingdom of God that is to be established
and made habitable among men.
You Crown the Year with Your Goodness, 207

The communion of saints thus has its origins in the redemptive Incarnation, life, suffering, death, and Resurrection of Jesus Christ. Citing Saint Thomas Aquinas,
Balthasar notes:

In the Church, therefore, all representative
being, acting and suffering [on behalf of others]
is founded on Christ's representative being,
acting and suffering.
Theo-Drama IV: The Action, 423n36

Balthasar points to Mary as the most profound exemplar,
after Jesus, of the communion of saints:

What we speak of as the "communion of saints",
that is, the interrelatedness and osmosis of human
destiny, has its origin in Christ, the bearer of all

guilt; but a profound element in Christ is the self-renouncing "Yes" of the Handmaid of the Lord [Mary], a "Yes" that creates a space accessible to all, where all may dwell and "plunder" its goods.

You Crown the Year with Your Goodness, 196

Because he has bestowed on us his Holy Spirit and given us his Body, Christ is the wellspring of the Communion of Saints, which is nothing other than the full power of every loving person to communicate to others in need his own store of divine gifts. And this is the essence of the whole work of redemption, which the Father has permitted and made possible through his goodness. But it is in Mary that we can best grasp what the Communion of Saints is for us men. For if each of God's gifts also contains his petition and demand that we should receive the gift and reciprocate it, it is in Mary that the correspondence between gift and self-giving, reception and thanksgiving attains perfection. This makes man capable of being fruitful along with the eternal fruitfulness of God, so that out of his completed self-surrender he can, in turn, form a gift and thus transmit the divine grace further through himself. Mary-the-Church keeps no grace for herself; she receives grace in order to transmit it. This is what a mother does. We are the children of Mary's fruitfulness, and her fruitfulness has been given her that she might receive and fulfill the fruitfulness of her Spouse.

And this obliges us, too, ourselves to be the
Church and to become inserted into this
cycle of reception and transmission.
The Threefold Garland, 136–37

The more perfectly a Christian develops this
selfless love in himself, the more all others can
live on his goods as if they were their own.
Not only are individuals transparent to one
another, they also radiate what is theirs into the
others—although we can speak only in a loose
sense of "theirs", because perfect selflessness and
transparency are nothing other than the life of
God and Christ in creatures. Mary, as the purest
of all creatures, irradiates what is her own least
of all. Everyone within the communion of
saints has something Marian about him.
Mary: The Church at the Source, 122

Balthasar often places special emphasis on the spiritual
fruit that is generated for the communion of saints via *sacrifices* that are willingly made and *suffering* (perhaps to the
point of death) that is willingly undergone and "offered
up" to God for the benefit of others:

It is when the heart renounces itself and
gives pride of place to the "thou", bearing
the other's burden and ready ultimately,
if it comes to it, to put the other person first,
that the communion of saints is realized.
You Crown the Year with Your Goodness, 218

In perfect renunciation lies unrestricted fruitfulness.
Light of the Word, 55

Even suffering, *particularly* suffering, is a precious
gift that the one suffering can hand on to others;
it helps, it purifies, it atones, it communicates
divine graces. The sufferings of a mother can
bring a wayward son back to the right path; the
sufferings of someone with cancer or leprosy,
if offered to God, can be a capital for God to
use, bearing fruit in the most unexpected places.
Suffering, accepted with thanksgiving and
handed on, participates in the great fruitfulness
of everything that streams from God's joy
and returns to him by circuitous paths.
You Crown the Year with Your Goodness, 30

The God-man's unique, soteriological *pro nobis*
["for us"; "in our place"] is communicated in
the mystery of the *communio sanctorum*, namely,
that those who believe and suffer can really
stand in one another's place.
Theo-Logic I: Truth of the World, 21

According to the laws of the communion
of saints, [a person] can offer himself to God
on behalf of other people (perhaps even for
quite specific people), by asking, suffering
and being *for them*.
Theo-Drama III: The Dramatis Personae:
The Person in Christ, 271n5

Recognizing his suffering as Christ's, and as
a grace, [a Christian] can enjoy the Christian
hope that—in however hidden a manner—
this suffering, in union with Christ's, will
promote the salvation of the world.
Theo-Drama V: The Last Act, 177

For the suffering and dying person himself, this meaning [of his suffering and dying] reaches beyond the confines of his own individual existence, since it can become a form of substitutionary suffering and expiation on behalf of mankind as a whole.

Explorations in Theology V: Man Is Created, 112

Since this love-death of our Lord, death has taken on a quite different meaning; it can become for us an expression of our purest and most living love, assuming that we take it as a conferred opportunity to give ourselves unreservedly into the hands of God. It is then not merely an atonement for everything that we failed to do, but, beyond that, an earning of grace for others to abandon their egoism and choose love as their innermost disposition.

Credo, 54

One prays, and makes one's sacrifices, and knows: prayer and sacrifice will "be of benefit" somewhere and sometime to "the soul". We may not know how this will happen, but we can rest in the knowledge that God will "use" all that is given. Those who suffer, and to whom their pain seems meaningless, must again and again be assured of this; how otherwise could they bear it? But what is meant here by "use"? Surely only that what is given is taken up into the great groundless giving of God as a wave is taken back into the sea. Or at least that one surrenders it and that God must do with it what he will.

Elucidations, 199–200

> One can speak of a genuine healing when
> a sufferer who was previously the slave
> of his suffering becomes its master, accepts
> it in inner freedom and, if he is a Christian,
> lets God manage and allot it.
> *New Elucidations*, 271

> What a hope for all earthly sufferers, who are
> usually unable to find any meaning in their
> suffering! It remains in God's keeping, and is,
> in God, in a mysterious way, fruitful.
> *Credo*, 97

Indeed, Balthasar maintains that suffering (and praying, too) can be as fruitful as, and perhaps even more fruitful than, external activity undertaken on the world's behalf:

> We have just mentioned the most important
> acts that are exchanged within the inner
> communion of the faithful: praying for others
> and suffering for others (besides, of course,
> the visible, external mutual help that is a
> matter of course for Christians). For [Saint]
> Paul, the former are at least as important as
> the external ministrations; indeed, they are
> basically more necessary and more effective,
> since they are more closely linked to Christ's
> "being-for", "acting-for" and "suffering-for".
> *Theo-Drama IV: The Action*, 421

So the Christian, too, can be confident: provided he rests in God, in prayer, in meditation, in self-surrender, in readiness to respond to God's

call, but also in suffering, incapable of engaging
in external works, he is actually working, even
without knowing it; he is collaborating with
God's tireless word and Spirit. He works through
being, not necessarily through *doing*, just as the
sun works simply through being there.

You Crown the Year with Your Goodness, 167

Suffering is good for something and has
an even greater efficacy than all the
achievements of the healthy.

Explorations in Theology V: Man Is Created, 285

All who suffer in this world, the sick
and incurable and dying, those in prison and
tortured, the oppressed and those who are
hopelessly poor, must know that, in their
situation, they are not condemned to total
powerlessness: if they unite their hopelessness
with that of the crucified Son of God, they
will do more to build the real kingdom of God
than many an architect of earthly happiness.

You Crown the Year with Your Goodness, 74

[Suffering and death] can receive more meaning
and bear more fruit than the greatest and
most successful activity, a meaning not only
for the one who suffers but precisely also
for others, for the world as a whole.

A Short Primer for Unsettled Laymen, 91

One side note: lest the reader think that Balthasar is rec-
ommending a "masochistic" attitude toward suffering, I
include the following:

Above all, we must not wish to cling to
our suffering. Suffering surely deepens us
and enhances our person, but we must not
desire to become a deeper self than God wills.
To suffer no longer can be a beautiful,
perhaps the ultimate, sacrifice.
The Grain of Wheat, 51

Where is the communion of saints to be found here on
earth? First and foremost, within the Church. The Church
and her members are to exemplify the love of the communion of saints and to engage in acts of love that generate
spiritual fruit for the benefit of others:

The Church must be the place where people
catch a glimpse of something of the mysterious
realm of love, of the communion of saints.
You Crown the Year with Your Goodness, 221

All charisms of Christians are inextricably
interwoven; everyone owes himself not
only to God but to the whole Church;
everyone is borne by invisible prayers and
sacrifices, has been nourished by countless
gifts of love, is continually strengthened
and preserved by the affection of others.
My Work: In Retrospect, 88

The bad things [that the Church and her members
have done] stick in the memory better than the
good, but also ... the Christian good [i.e., the
good that Christians do] is either not at all or only
very indirectly apparent to the world. For who
can number and weigh the many hidden acts of

self-mastery through which evil is averted, who
the acts of selfless reparation and loving solicitude,
or who, indeed, the power of secret, fervent
prayers? Who but God knows the experiences of
the saints who have been through heaven and hell
and who, from the most hidden of places, have
changed the entire course of historical events,
moved whole mountains of guilt, and opened
a passageway in hopeless situations? Let this be
merely noted here, in passing and sotto voce,
in order to remind ourselves that the debit side
of the Church's reckoning cannot be
computed without including this credit.

Who Is a Christian?, 17

People who are called by Jesus Christ to a religious vocation within the Church (for example, as priest, sister, religious, etc.) are especially called to pour themselves out
eucharistically in order to generate spiritual fruit for the
communio sanctorum:

Christ calls those he especially chooses to
live an "ecclesial existence" at the very heart
of the Church. Whether exteriorly or interiorly,
visibly or in a hidden manner, he calls them
to become fruitful a hundredfold and to
distribute themselves Eucharistically in the
mysteries of the communion of saints.

Explorations in Theology II: Spouse of the Word, 439

However, the *communio sanctorum* is not restricted to the
"visible Church"; it extends to all human beings, both
past and present, because Jesus Christ suffered and died on
behalf of all mankind:

The reality of the *communio sanctorum* with its
mysterious laws whereby each can "be for" others
through prayer, initiative and suffering on their
behalf [is not] restricted to the realm of the visible
Church: it reaches as far as Christ's merits extend.
Theo-Drama III: The Dramatis Personae:
The Person in Christ, 281–82

Men, who together form "one dough" (Gregory
of Nyssa) or "one cake" (Luther), can be, act,
and suffer much more profoundly for one
another than they often think.
Theo-Logic II: Truth of God, 232

No mortal eye can mark the boundaries of the
communion of saints. For no one knows how far
love is able to radiate, how much it can sustain
and act on behalf of others. All sinners are borne
up and revalued in the power of love of Jesus
Christ's heart, whether they know it or not,
whether they accept it or not.
You Crown the Year with Your Goodness, 221

Thus, Balthasar asserts that believers can, out of love, act
on behalf of nonbelievers:

The believer believes for the nonbelievers;
he receives Communion for the
noncommunicants because the body
he receives has borne the sins of all.
Life Out of Death, 67

Such a man will pray out of gratitude to God
and out of responsibility for his fellow men.

He will not pay a great deal of attention to his
own feelings or lack of feelings, to the extent to
which he experiences God's presence or absence.
Perhaps he will be allowed to feel the absent
God of those who do not pray, in order that
the latter may catch an intimation of the God
who is present. Such things are given within the
communio sanctorum, which in the widest sense is
the community of all those for whom God on the
Cross has borne and suffered total abandonment.
And that indeed is everyone.
Elucidations, 180

The "merit", therefore, is exclusively at
Christ's service, although, in handing it over,
the Christian may link it with some quite
specific request or intention. Everything passes
through Christ's and God's freedom, and this
prevents any direct experience—let alone
calculation—of cause and effect.
In the Fullness of Faith, 72

The one thus loving cannot foresee the
full implications of her action but simply
surrenders her attempt to love to the Love
of God, to use it as he will. But God uses it for
his own ends, which man cannot fathom and
whose revelation (now or on the Last Day)
will astonish him as the highest beatitude.
Who Is a Christian?, 75

How far does the power of intercession for
another extend? How far can we act on behalf

of someone else? Is it possible to win the grace
of conversion for a person in grave sin?... [A]ll
that is hidden from us is the mechanism by
which the members of the Body can act on
behalf of one another. God alone can know this.
But it gives us a firm hope that the energies of
this 'acting on behalf of others' can affect the
innermost regions of others' freedom.
Theo-Drama IV: The Action, 412

There is in principle no limit to the possible
influence of one member upon another
within the spiritual community of goods,
both in space and time.
Theo-Drama IV: The Action, 413

[In the communion of saints] all the good
things are poured out infinitely over everyone,
shared out among everyone. The tiniest act
of genuine, self-denying love comes from
God's eternity and so must continue to
transmit its effect through all eternity.
You Crown the Year with Your Goodness, 222

What a beautiful and meaningful life, in which every act
of love, no matter how small, radiates into eternity for the
benefit of others!

Part III

Some Types of Love

In this section of the book, we will reflect upon some of Balthasar's insights regarding the following types of love: love of God, love of neighbor, sexual love, filial love, and self-love.

7

Give Me Your Heart: Loving God

In discussing human beings' love for God, Balthasar emphasizes the primacy (or what theologians often refer to as the "prevenience") of God's love for us: "In this is love, not that we loved God but that he loved us" (1 Jn 4:10). God's love for us came first, and God hopes that we will use the freedom he gave us to love him in return. God has willed each of us, loved each of us, into existence, and he sustains us in being every moment of our lives. Our love for God is, at the most fundamental level, a response to that ongoing gift of life and love:

> Already to exist is a work of love!
> *Heart of the World*, 26–27

> Love desires no recompense other than to be
> loved in return; and thus God desires nothing in
> return for his love for us other than our love.
> *Love Alone Is Credible*, 107

But of course God has done far more than loving us into existence and sustaining us in existence every moment of our lives; God has given the complete gift of himself to us in Jesus Christ, and this self-gift invites the response on our part of a total gift of self back to God:

Through the distinct operations of each of
the three Persons [of the Trinity], the world
acquires an inward share in the divine exchange
of life; as a result the world is able to take
the divine things it has received from God,
together with the gift of being created, and
return them to God as a divine gift.
Theo-Drama V: The Last Act, 521

For God does not give us just something: he gives
us himself, his heart, his word, his mind. And
what he requires from us, in response, is not
just something but the entire investment of
our selves, our binding word, our heart.
You Crown the Year with Your Goodness, 229

Basically, in Jesus Christ's death, Descent into
Hell and Resurrection, only one reality is there
to be seen: the love of the triune God for the
world, a love which can only be perceived
through a co-responsive love.
Mysterium Paschale, 262

[Man's] gift of self is a response, to the one who
is the ground of his being-permitted-to-be; to
him who ultimately wants from man not things
and objects but his very self. *Fili, praebe mihi
cor tuum.* [Son, give me your heart.]
*The Glory of the Lord V:
The Realm of Metaphysics in the Modern Age,* 654

Balthasar, addressing Jesus, cleverly reverses Saint Augus-
tine's famous formula that our hearts are restless until they
rest in God, in order to emphasize Jesus' desire for our love:

Your Heart is restless until it rests in me. Your
Heart is restless until we rest in you, once time
and eternity have become interfused.
Heart of the World, 219

Echoing Saint Thérèse of Lisieux, Balthasar makes the
seemingly extravagant claim that God "urgently needs"
our love:

God wishes to be loved. God urgently needs
the creature to demonstrate his love and pour
upon him the free stream of his love.
Two Sisters in the Spirit, 271

In another passage, Balthasar describes Jesus as a "beggar
for [our] love":

[Jesus] desires nearness; he would like to
live in you and commingle his breath with
your breathing. He would like to be with
you until the end of the world. He knocks
at all the souls.... He seeks trust, intimacy;
he is a beggar for your love.
Heart of the World, 120–21

Such descriptions of God's desire for our love could, to a
certain extent, be called hyperbole, for God is perfect in
himself and has no "need" of our love in any sense of there
being a lack or an imperfection in God's state of being that
only the love of human beings can address. Nonetheless,
this dramatic language is solidly based in the Bible, which
speaks repeatedly of God's love for human beings being so
great that God desires a "marriage" between himself and

all human beings. Balthasar uses or refers to this conjugal imagery in several passages; here are a representative few:

> Even in the Old Testament God offers man
> an inconceivably intimate relationship with
> him. Just think of the image of conjugal union
> employed by Hosea, Jeremiah and Ezekiel.
> God, the All-Holy, wishes to join himself
> to the continually unfaithful and adulterous
> Israel, as if to a prostitute.
>
> *You Crown the Year with Your Goodness*, 151

> The "bodily" union of humanity with God made
> present to it has been, in a manner beyond all
> comprehension, presented to us in terms of *eros*,
> as the fulfillment of what the Song of Songs had
> celebrated long before: existence as a bridal state.
>
> *A Theology of History*, 122

> [The Church] Fathers, in particular Ambrose,
> saw the formation of the hypostatic union [the
> union of the divine nature and human nature in
> the Incarnation of Jesus Christ] as the real and
> primordial marriage union, that of God with the
> whole of mankind.... [T]he marriage of Christ
> and the Church is to be interpreted only against
> the background of an, as it were, fundamental
> marriage with mankind as a whole.
>
> *Explorations in Theology II: Spouse of the Word*, 181

> The Church is not an abstract collective
> or a "moral subject", but the profoundly
> mysterious reality of a second Eve
> formed for a second Adam.
>
> *The Moment of Christian Witness*, 44

God is ceaselessly wooing man in the
Person of the Crucified.
Theo-Drama V: The Last Act, 478

[Jesus speaking:] Between every soul and me
there is this covenant, this virginal bond
of holy marriage. For each one, I am the
whole, the utmost, the unconditional.
I am father, mother, friend and spouse.
Heart of the World, 167

The miracle of [Jesus'] Eucharist: he is in
you and you are in him—a wedding-feast
without end between you and him, compared
with which the union of man and wife
is but a brief and poor effort.
Heart of the World, 128

The whole progress of the world points to
there being a creator whose purpose is to
bring about, by means of his creative powers,
a free response from his creatures below, so
that they may move toward him and finally be
united with him in a marriage of love.
The Moment of Christian Witness, 76

Ideally, our love for God progresses from a love that is
mainly self-focused (*erós*, in which we love God primarily
because of the ways in which God fulfills our needs) to
one that is selfless (*caritas*, in which we love God for God's
own sake, or, in other words, in which we love the absolute Good because of his goodness and not just because
of the good things we receive from him). In the following passages, Balthasar describes this transition, referring to
some of the philosophers in Antiquity (primarily Plato and

Plotinus) who had inklings of this process and to some of
the Christian thinkers who deepened and developed our
understanding of this process:

> Already with Plato and Plotinus it has been shown
> that in its highest manifestation eros is thought of
> as self-less, because it loves the Good for the sake
> of the Good, so that it can become a reflection
> of the highest Good, radiating like the sun
> freely and gratuitously. This vision overwhelms
> the Christian [Marsilio] Ficino and makes him
> interpret all being as beauty, for he sees in it the
> gracious self-radiation of the Good, deepened
> in a Christian sense as eternal love.
>
> *The Glory of the Lord V:*
> *The Realm of Metaphysics in the Modern Age,* 253

> [Jean Pierre de] Caussade regards it as self-evident
> that this surrender [to God] should demand
> [François] Fénelon's *amour pur* [pure love]:
> "Were we to love God a little for the sake
> of His gifts, He would be loved for His own
> sake when the gift was no longer noticed."
> And "if the divine goodness does not require
> us to despise the happiness for which we are
> destined, it surely has the right to be loved for
> its own sake without any regard of our own
> interests". That is well said and corresponds to
> the metaphysics of the saints in every century.
>
> *The Glory of the Lord V:*
> *The Realm of Metaphysics in the Modern Age,* 139

Obviously, this is setting the bar very high. Since we are
creatures, our love for God will, at least most of the time, be

more of what C.S. Lewis (1898–1963) refers to as "Need-love" rather than "Gift-love",[1] but hopefully, through grace, we can experience moments, at least occasionally, where our love for God reaches the heights of loving God for his own sake, of loving the absolute Good because he is goodness itself and not merely out of our own desire for the good.

One final topic for reflection in this chapter, which will also serve as our transition to the next chapter on the love of neighbor: In his discussion of the two greatest commandments (love of God and love of neighbor: Matthew 22:34–40; Mark 12:28–34; Luke 10:25–28), Balthasar rightly rejects the tendency on the part of some recent thinkers to claim that love of neighbor is enough—that we do not need to believe in and love God as long as we love our neighbor. We are certainly called to love our neighbor (by working for social justice, for example), but this love does not substitute for believing in and loving God:

> Anyone who proclaims the identity of the love of
> God and one's neighbor and presents the love of
> one's neighbor as the primary meaning of the love
> of God must not be surprised (and doubtless is not)
> if it becomes a matter of indifference whether he
> professes to believe in [and love] God or not.
>
> *The Moment of Christian Witness*, 120

> The dissolution of the love of God into
> the love of neighbour ... would be the
> formation of a "Christian atheism".
>
> *The Glory of the Lord VII: Theology:*
> *The New Covenant*, 441

[1] C.S. Lewis, *The Four Loves* (San Francisco: HarperOne, 2017), 3–4. Josef Pieper seconds Lewis on this and elaborates upon this point in his book *Faith, Hope, Love* (San Francisco: Ignatius Press, 1997), 221–22.

Balthasar speaks eloquently of the intimate connection between love of God and love of neighbor and the synergistic way in which these two loves feed back on each other and find their ultimate unity in Christ:

> John [the Evangelist] draws us into the circuit of love that sets up such a pulsing flow between love for God and love for neighbor that each of these loves lives, is effective, and derives validity from the other. In the process he frees us from our doubts about our love. Do I love my neighbor? Yes, if I love God. Do I love God? Yes, if I love my neighbor. Yet the energy powering this circuit comes from the unity of both poles in Jesus Christ, who lived out the love of the Father toward mankind at the same time he lived out human love for the Father. Only if one shares in Christ through immersion in his birth from the Father and in Christ's world mission, rather than through some purely theoretical faith, will our faith close the circuit together with Christ, permitting the power to flow. All of this is said clearly in 1 John 5:1–6.... And thus the circuit of love between God and man is completed in Christ.
> *You Have Words of Eternal Life*, 190, 192

> Since God's Word is now made man, we can encounter the embodied Word of God itself in our fellowman—not only can, but ... actually do. Through God's Incarnation in Jesus, in fact, love of God and love of neighbor fuse for the first time into the object of [a] single commandment.
> *Explorations in Theology V: Man Is Created*, 445

8

The Sacrament of Christ:
Loving Our Neighbor

In our love for our "neighbor" (which includes *all* of our
fellow human beings), we are called to imitate Jesus' gift
of self to the world:

> Jesus' gift of self becomes the
> model for our imitation.
> *Mysterium Paschale,* 111

> God ... is love that flows out to men in his
> Son: man is required to fit himself into
> the rhythm of this movement.
> *The Glory of the Lord VII: Theology:*
> *The New Covenant,* 454

> The presence of perfect self-giving
> [in Jesus Christ] ... is now the definitive
> model of ethical human action.
> *Theo-Drama II: The Dramatis Personae: Man in God,* 123

In the eyes of the world, the "greater" person is the one
who possesses more wealth, wields more power, and/or
holds a position of higher prestige in the social hierarchy
than others. Jesus turns this judgment on its head; the

"greater" person is actually the one who loves, and therefore serves, more deeply than others, even to the point of loving his enemies:

> The "greater", more Christian person is
> the person who serves more deeply; like
> Jesus, who serves at the eucharistic table and
> washes the feet of his enemy, Judas.
> *New Elucidations*, 238

> As Christians ... we no longer live merely
> alongside one another, but, since we are part
> of the body of Christ, also, in a sense, inside
> one another; and indeed, not only with a group,
> not only with a communion or church, but
> with all those for whom Christ surrendered
> himself, in expiation, for the forgiveness of sins.
> No one is excepted from this. Therefore, a
> Christian does not know the word "enemy".
> *Credo*, 92

Imitating Jesus' loving self-gift ranges all the way from "simple, anonymous acts of love" up to the ultimate self-gift, giving one's life for one's neighbor:

> [Jesus] aligns himself with those who do
> simple, anonymous acts of love. Who can
> know precisely where in the wide world
> all the many such acts of self-giving take place?
> Where someone gives greater weight to his
> neighbor than to his own importance? Such
> things remain in the mystery of God.
> *Who Is a Christian?*, 99–100

[Only he who loves] is able to respond
selflessly when another confides in and
opens up to him, perhaps seeks his help,
questions him, or calls to him.
Theo-Logic I: Truth of the World, 112

[The Christian's] duty is to experience
the presence of absolute love, and himself to
actualise it, and to make it visible, within his
love for his neighbour; it is his task to effect
the miracle of the multiplication of the loaves
precisely out of this poverty ("What is that for
so many?"). His faith teaches him to see within
the most seemingly unimportant interpersonal
relation the making present and the "sacrament"
of the eternal I-Thou relation.
The Glory of the Lord V:
The Realm of Metaphysics in the Modern Age, 649

In the Bible, perfect love is not a counsel but a
command; moreover, it comes across more and
more clearly and challengingly as the one and
only command, which, in the sight of God, gives
meaning to all other precepts. Without love
they would all be nothing but police regulations
designed to prevent the coexisting predators
from devouring each other at will.
You Crown the Year with Your Goodness, 218–19

The commandment of love does not just go for a
few steps. Since it is proclaimed in the face of the
Cross and its vicarious suffering, it demands a total
engagement, the willingness to go along on the
path one is forced to travel (Mt 5:41), to the point

of hanging with the other, even unto hanging in
the other's stead (Rom 9:3). Christian joy in its
totality wells up from this point of solidarity.
The Christian and Anxiety, 93

Christianity's core concept is found in the
Lord's "new commandment" to love one's
neighbor as oneself, indeed, more than
oneself, since no one has greater love than
the one who gives his life for his friends (Jn
15:13), yes, even for his enemies (Rom 5:10).
The Christian and Anxiety, 93

What then should a Christian be? He should
be one who offers up his life in the service
of his fellow man because he owes his
life to Christ crucified.
The Moment of Christian Witness, 133

Thus the idea that someone could seriously
be concerned for his own eternal salvation
without being equally concerned for the eternal
salvation of his brother and neighbor (and who
is *not* my neighbor?)—this is not only an un-
Christian idea: it is also an inhuman idea.
You Crown the Year with Your Goodness, 218

I must be able to hope for every brother so
much that ... if it were a question of whether he
or I were to enter into the Kingdom of God, I
would—with Paul (Rom 9:3)—let him go.
The Moment of Christian Witness, 126

How could we ever find it possible to love other people,
especially people in whom we may not initially see much,

if anything, that is "loveable", in such a profoundly self-sacrificial way? In part, by seeing Christ in every other person and keeping in mind that Christ died for the sake of everyone else's salvation just as he did for ours:

In his plight and guilt, our fellow-man as we encounter him is in every case our neighbour, and this neighbour of man's is Christ. In his neighbour man encounters his Redeemer with all his bodily senses, in just as concrete, unprecedented, and archetypal a manner as the Apostles when they "found the Messiah" (Jn 1.41).
The Glory of the Lord I: Seeing the Form, 414

That is why we can speak of our brother, not as "Christ in disguise", but as the "sacrament of Christ". [Christ] infallibly communicates his presence under these signs; thus he can be genuinely found and encountered. For the believer, the myriad forms of relationships between human beings can become so many ways of encountering Christ, each one new, original and surprising.
Prayer, 215

[Jesus' sacrifice for all people] changes everything, for from now on, one's fellow-man—whether friend or foe—is "the brother for whom Christ died" (1 Cor 8.11; Rom 14.15), and whoever sins against his brother sins against Christ (1 Cor 8.12).
The Glory of the Lord VII: Theology:
The New Covenant, 439

We must learn from the very beginning not to use our natural eyes when looking at our neighbor,

nor the categories of everyday psychology as the
measure of his worth. Rather must we look at
him "with the eyes of faith" so that we may
see him as God sees him in Jesus Christ.
Engagement with God, 51

We can look at our neighbor in this way
only in the closest possible reliance upon
God, in prayer, and in self-denial.
Theo-Logic I: Truth of the World, 271

The eyes of Christian love are full of faith and
of faith's contemplation; they have a luminosity
which discovers and lights up a supernatural depth
in whatever and whomsoever they fasten upon: this
sinner, this unattractive and insignificant person,
this avowed opponent of the Church and of Jesus
Christ is in reality my brother; Jesus has borne his
sins just as he has borne mine (which means that
there can be no accusations on either side); his
unpleasant characteristics are a burden he is obliged,
willy-nilly, to drag around with him, and although
I cannot see it, this burden has some connection,
through God's grace, with the total burden which
weighs on the shoulders of Jesus Christ.
Prayer, 216

Others ... are also children born of eternal
love and thus endlessly lovable.
You Have Words of Eternal Life, 190

We spend a whole life long awaiting the arrival of
the extraordinary person, instead of transforming
the ordinary people around us into such.
The Grain of Wheat, 111

Occasionally, Balthasar expands his discussion of love of neighbor to a global scale, noting that the best response to the problems besetting the world today is that of selfless love, a love that extends even to one's "enemies":

> The modern technological world may have tremendous problems that seem utterly remote from the Gospel, but ultimately it comes down to the attitude adopted by Jesus in his living and dying: the attitude of perfect, selfless love, service to the very last and the fruitfulness that comes from it. This is the innermost meaning and core of all mankind's questions, including those of politics, economics and other fields. And the attitude shown by Jesus is the attitude of God himself to the world. Thus anyone who follows Jesus is walking in God's footsteps, in the footsteps of absolute truth and goodness.
>
> *You Crown the Year with Your Goodness*, 255

The path to the goal ... is a walking in the power of love. The problems of mankind are so difficult to solve—industrialization, the conservation of resources, the distribution of goods, world food provision—but unless we are grounded in love, unless we start from love, they will only become more and more intractable. Love must penetrate even into the hardest realism of economics and politics if we are not to perish at one another's hand. In John we read, "he who hates his brother is a murderer", and Jesus spoke in very similar terms in the Sermon on the Mount. There are entire nations, and great nations, who bring up

their children to hate the others, the "enemies",
and it is only a question of time before these
latent murderous energies come out into the
public arena. The fuse is already burning at the
powder keg. Yet ... there are still the mysterious
interstices, the in-between spaces: there, by God's
appointment, dwell those who desire to live in
and for his love. They keep the world going.
They cannot be ascertained statistically, for,
according to Jesus' word, the kingdom of
God is not coming with "signs to be observed"
(Lk 17:20). Such people can live on either side
of the totalitarian frontier, on either side of
the barbed wire. Nor can their influence be
completely assessed; often the best of it remains
hidden. They are like subterranean springs and
streams that moisten the roots from below.

You Crown the Year with Your Goodness, 25

Love of one's enemies as the axial
element—and not just as an incidental
act of heroism—is Christian agape in
the form appropriate for our time.

Explorations in Theology II: Spouse of the Word, 34

We who are trying to follow [Jesus], we will
work with all our power to promote the
Kingdom of God, justice between men, but first
of all by changing the dispositions of hearts, by
opening them to those of the Heart of Jesus.

To the Heart of the Mystery of Redemption, 60–61

It is exclusively in this realm of the heart, hidden
or somehow made manifest, that mankind's

real progress takes place; this is where the great decisions of history are made, the destructive forces are defeated and the constructive forces are set loose, giving us grounds for something like hope. Only this realm of the heart can determine the sphere of validity of works of culture as well as of the secular, rational technology that produces machines and is produced by them; it is this realm of the heart that weighs and assesses them.

You Crown the Year with Your Goodness, 213

Faith, hope and love are what the Bridegroom [Jesus Christ] knows, what he desires, for it is his own mind and heart; nor will there be any other disposition in God's heaven but this. Then all the other things that seem big and important on earth will be played out: science, technology, power. But the other three, as the Apostle assures us, will abide forever, and the greatest of them is love. For only the man who loves God really believes in him and hopes in him. In the kingdom of God love will be the attitude governing everything.

You Crown the Year with Your Goodness, 259

9

Bodily Things Communicated Spiritually, Spiritual Things Communicated Bodily: Sexual Love

When the Adam of Genesis fails to find a
partner among the animals, it is not because
he lacks communication from spirit to spirit:
what he misses is the relationship in which
bodily things are communicated spiritually
and spiritual things bodily.

Theo-Drama II: The Dramatis Personae: Man in God, 366

Balthasar does not discuss sexual love at great length, but
there are at least two themes that can be extracted from
his writings for our reflection: the beauty and goodness of
sexual love within the context of marriage, and the extent
of self-giving required by marriage.

With regard to the first theme, Balthasar applauds what
has come to be referred to as the "Theology of the Body"
formulated by Saint John Paul II, a theology that affirms
the beauty and goodness of our bodies and our sexuality,
in contrast to schools of thought in the course of human
history that have deprecated the body and sexuality:

I consider [Saint John Paul II's] thoughts
concerning the body of the highest importance,
because the subject has always been, and still
is, surrounded by forms of Platonism and
spiritualism, which disparage the body and
everything material in favor of a pure spirituality.
Test Everything: Hold Fast to What Is Good, 80

Balthasar emphasizes the beauty and the significance of
sexual love by noting that it points toward the depth of
God's love for us and also serves as an image of the union
between God and human beings that is our intended destiny. He contrasts the high esteem with which Christianity
regards our sexuality with the increasingly casual attitude
toward sex on the part of secular society:

Erotic love is not a lower form of love or a
distant parable for God's love for the land
which he now refers to as "espoused" and "my
delight". Natural, human love should be a point
of departure by which men can sense how much
they are loved by God. Indeed, the sexual union
of husband and wife becomes an, admittedly
inadequate, image of the intimate union between
Christ and us in the holy Eucharist.
Light of the Word, 270

Since the establishment of the covenant with
Israel and a fortiori since the Incarnation of the
Son of God and the institution of his Eucharist,
sexual intercourse can only be interpreted—
in a fully Christian sense—as a pointer to the
"one flesh" that exists between Christ and

Church, Heaven and earth. The more
insignificant it becomes for the world, the
more precious it is to Christians.
In the Fullness of Faith, 113–14

This fundamental relationship makes man, in
the reciprocity of husband and wife, an image
and a likeness of God: of the God who, in his
eternal trinitarian mystery, already possesses
within himself a nuptial form.
The Glory of the Lord I: Seeing the Form, 560–61

As in all of the other aspects of love upon which we have
been reflecting, Jesus' self-giving is the paradigm for the
self-giving and self-surrender that we are called to in married love:

[Jesus'] offering of flesh and blood on the Cross
and remaining in the Eucharist is a parable, better
yet, the archetype of all married self-giving.
Light of the Word, 242

For Christians, marriage is a sacrament, which
means above all a form, given as a gift to the
spouses, of following Christ in his fruitful,
purifying, complete self-surrender to his
spouse, the Church. The Christian attitude
and practice of married life receive their
norm from here (Eph 5:22–33).
A Short Primer for Unsettled Laymen, 78

This grace [the grace given by God to spouses
in the sacrament of marriage] has the nature
of a self-renouncing love: husband and wife

offer up to each other their rule over their
own bodies (1 Cor 7:4); the wife becomes
the husband's "own flesh", and his self-love
becomes love for her (Eph 5:28).
The Moment of Christian Witness, 48

The union of husband and wife means more
than merely physical fruitfulness, the begetting
of children; it means spiritual fruitfulness
as well, total surrender to each other.
New Elucidations, 223

[Saint Paul] places [marriage] expressly under
the norm of Christ's love for his bride, for
humanity redeemed by him. The man, even
and specifically in the sexual act, must show
perfect, loving self-giving, which at the same
time takes up the self-giving of the woman and
gives it form; the wife is the one who allows
herself to be formed, without setting inner
limits on the love which she has received. In
the opposition of the sexes, which in none of
its aspects is simply physical but which always
leaves its imprint on personal attitudes and
responses, lies the possibility of a perfect mutual
interpenetration which opens up the way to
a unity of love and to a fruitfulness which
transcends the two individual partners.
Elucidations, 224–25

What else is [Jesus'] Eucharist but, at a higher
level, an endless act of fruitful outpouring of his
whole flesh, such as a man can achieve only for

a moment with a limited organ of his body? And
the man soon withdraws again into himself, and
it is only rarely that his heart fully achieves the
meaning of the physical act: the letting oneself go
completely, the handing over of oneself totally
in a love which "does not seek his own", which
seeks neither pleasure nor gain for itself. It is only
rarely that he understands that the mark of his
sexuality in his body is a reminder of his own
dispossession: You are there in order that you may
become fruitful beyond yourself, in an act of self-
giving which alone reveals what you can properly
achieve: namely, procreation in the freedom and
power of your Creator. The physical is only a
pointer to something which equally determines
his whole personality, his spiritual life.
Elucidations, 226

All human relationships are characterized by
elements of self-revelation within a context
of mystery. This is what makes them valuable
and thrilling—which applies to the most
intimate exchanges in sexual intercourse, too,
if it is the expression of genuine personal love.
Communicating the incommunicable: this
paradox is nowhere more evident than here.
Nor is it a tragic mystery, either: it is a mystery
full of bliss and promise. My partner must be
allowed room in which to reveal himself freely,
as both "I" and "Thou", so that he can give
himself and be accepted by me.
Truth Is Symphonic, 31–32

Balthasar openly acknowledges the difficulties and challenges of living out the high calling to self-giving love in marriage, noting that doing so will require "many renunciations" but will also yield "the only true happiness", the happiness produced by entering into the divine movement of self-giving love:

> For sexuality as Christians understand it—
> sexuality that takes as its norm the relationship
> between Christ and his Church—Christ's words
> hold true: "Let him grasp it who can." But
> Christ is saying something more here than that
> very few men and women will actually grasp his
> doctrine. He is issuing us a challenge to serious
> endeavor, the same challenge, essentially, that
> rings through the whole of the Gospel: take up
> your cross every day, sell all you possess, and
> do not cheat as did Ananias and Sapphira [Acts
> 5:1–11]. Why should the sexual area alone offer
> no challenge to the Christian? Sexuality, even
> as *eros*, is to be an expression of *agape*, and *agape*
> always involves an element of renunciation. And
> only by renunciation can the limits that we set on
> our own self-surrender be transcended. I think
> that only Christians can understand the challenge
> posed by *Humanae Vitae*, and even Christians only
> to the degree that they strive to follow Christ as
> married persons, and keep his example before
> their eyes with ever-increasing devotion.
> *New Elucidations*, 227–28

Christian sexual ethics is best advised to keep to the quite simple outline of the New Testament.

For this is as unchangeable as the nature of
the divine love which has become flesh in
Christ.... So long as the Christian's heart and
mind are spellbound by this humble and totally
selfless love, he has in his possession the best
possible compass for finding his way in the fog
of sexual matters. With the image of this love
before him he will not be able to maintain that
the ideal of self-giving—of true self-giving,
not of throwing oneself in front of people—is
unrealistic in our world and impracticable. It
demands a very great deal: namely, to subordinate
everything to the love which does not seek its
own; but it gives a great deal more: namely, the
only true happiness. One can use sex, like drugs
and alcohol, to maneuver oneself into a state of
excited, illusory happiness, but one is merely
transporting oneself into momentary states which
do not alter one's nature or one's heart. The
states fade and disappear, and the heart finds itself
emptier and more loveless than before.

Elucidations, 231–32

The Christian task lies in trying to deepen
the erotic faculty from the surface of the
senses into the depths of the heart: for here
eros can keep alive an awed amazement at
one's partner's self-surrender within all the
routine of the common life, even after the
first sensual stimulus has evaporated.

Unless You Become Like This Child, 47

In marriage ... a great effort is needed to
refine the earthly *eros* so that it may become
a pure expression of heavenly *agape*. By the
power of Christ's grace, and sacramental grace
in particular, this effort can achieve its goal,
but not without many renunciations, which
lead, again, from the sphere of the proclamation
of the gospel to that of the Cross.
New Elucidations, 185

Eros and Agape are neither identical nor contrary.
For Eros is capable of understanding the meaning
of Agape and subordinating itself to it by
undergoing a death and a resurrection.
The Grain of Wheat, 97

[Married couples] will have no easy life if
they desire to make the absolute love of
Christ and his Church the rule of their lives.
But this love itself will guide the couple
along a path they can follow.
New Elucidations, 225

10

Imago Trinitatis: Filial Love

In discussing the love between parents and their children, Balthasar seeks to revive a beautiful image of the family that goes back at least to the time of Saint Bonaventure (1221–1274): the family as *imago Trinitatis* (image of the Holy Trinity):

> Bonaventure reflects explicitly on the
> love between man and woman [and the
> procreation of a child as the fruit of that love]
> as an image for the common production of the
> Holy Spirit by the Father and the Son.
> *Theo-Logic II: Truth of God*, 167–68

> The Holy Spirit who descends upon the
> Church is the Spirit of Jesus Christ as well as
> of God the Father. In other words, the Holy
> Spirit is the Spirit of the reciprocity of their
> love that reaches the point of complete
> interpenetration, a love that simultaneously
> bears its fruit, namely, the third Person in God.
> In the created order we have a distant analogy
> in the fact that married love between a man and
> a woman bears fruit in a child; every child is

> physical proof of consummated love, he is
> the "one body" formed by his parents.
>
> *Light of the Word*, 86–87

> If the child could come about solely as the
> result of the reciprocal love of man and woman
> (without a physical act), the similarity to the
> procession of the Spirit from the Father and the
> Son would be even more perfect.
>
> *Theo-Logic II: Truth of God*, 168n37

Balthasar considers the filial relationship to be the best image of the Holy Trinity to be found in all of creation, and he laments that theologians have not given more attention to this image of the family:

> The [parent-child] relationship ... remains,
> in spite of all the obvious dissimilarities, the
> most eloquent *imago Trinitatis* that we find
> woven into the fabric of the creature.
>
> *Theo-Logic II: Truth of God*, 62

> It is a cause for amazement that in discussions
> of trinitarian logic in the world the parent-child
> relationship is always lightly brushed aside.
>
> *Theo-Logic II: Truth of God*, 59

This is starting to change somewhat, however. Theologians are starting to devote more attention to this image of the family, perhaps partly in response to Balthasar's discussion of this concept. Marc Cardinal Ouellet, for example, has written a recent book about the family as *imago Trinitatis*.[1]

---

[1] Marc Cardinal Ouellet, *Divine Likeness: Toward a Trinitarian Anthropology of the Family* (Grand Rapids, Mich.: Eerdmans, 2006).

A second emphasis in Balthasar's writings about filial love is the crucial importance of the establishment of a loving bond between an infant and a loving caregiver (typically, the child's mother).[2] Balthasar asserts that the experience of this bond begins to awaken the child to love, to self-consciousness, to the transcendental aspects of being (beauty, goodness, truth, and unity), and to God:

> The infant is brought to consciousness of himself only by love, by the smile of his mother. In that encounter, the horizon of all unlimited being opens itself for him, revealing four things to him: (1) that he is one in love with the mother, even in being other than his mother, therefore all being is one; (2) that that love is good, therefore all Being is good; (3) that that love is true, therefore all Being is true; and (4) that that love evokes joy, therefore all Being is beautiful.
>
> *My Work: In Retrospect*, 114

> Now this is the true miracle among all these miracles of the beginning: that one day the mother's smile is recognized by the child as a sign of his acceptance in the world and that the center of his own self is disclosed to him as he returns the smile. He finds himself because he has been found.
>
> *Life Out of Death*, 13

> The developing human being ... is intrinsically ordered to "being *with*" [*Mitsein*] other men, so much so that he awakens to self-consciousness

---

[2] Joseph Cardinal Ratzinger and Hans Urs von Balthasar, *Mary: The Church at the Source*, trans. Adrian Walker (San Francisco: Ignatius Press, 2005), 102.

only through other human beings, normally
through his mother. In the mother's smile, it
dawns on him that there is a world into which
he is accepted and in which he is welcome, and
it is in this primordial experience that he becomes
aware of himself for the first time.... Long
before the child learns to speak, a mute dialogue
unfolds between mother and child on the basis
of the "being with" that is constitutive of
every conscious human being.
Mary: The Church at the Source, 102–3

No human "I" can awaken to itself unless
it is called "thou" by some other "I".
Theo-Drama II: The Dramatis Personae: Man in God, 286

In his description of the impact of the relationship between a loving caregiver and the infant, Balthasar refers to
many of the aspects of love upon which we have already
reflected, including sacrifice, suffering, openness, *ekstasis*,
and the gift of self:

Every pregnancy that is lived in a genuinely
human way includes a certain intercession, a
certain suffering on behalf of the child on the
way that is given to him at his birth as an invisible
present of grace to take on the journey through
life. It is a selfless hope, a commending to God
or—if one does not know God—to the invisible
powers that guide the fate of men and women.
Mary for Today, 24

A mother does not only give her flesh and blood
to the child but also something of her soul and

spirit. And this continues after the child is born,
as the child is nourished and brought up.
You Crown the Year with Your Goodness, 268

The "I" of the child is not created by the
mother but only brought out of a latency,
out of a state of being closed in on itself,
into its true being and openness.
Explorations in Theology III: Creator Spirit, 39

No single man can attain his true freedom
unless he is borne by the power of men's
openness to one another in love.
A Theological Anthropology, 88

The child awakes to genuine freedom only
through his parents' sacrificial self-denial.
Theo-Logic III: The Spirit of Truth, 242

The ... awakening of a child to the awareness of
self ... is accomplished only by the prompting
of a person[3] who, through his care, his love, his
smile, demonstrates to the child that there is a
world outside of him that can be trusted; and
it is this risk of going out of oneself [*ekstasis*]
that engenders the awareness of self.
To the Heart of the Mystery of Redemption, 50–51

The little child awakens to self-consciousness
through being addressed by the love of his
mother.... The interpretation of the mother's
smiling and of her whole gift of self is the answer,

---

[3] Note that in this passage, Balthasar does not limit the role of a loving caregiver in the child's life to the mother.

awakened by her, of love to love, when the "I"
is addressed by the "Thou"; and precisely because
it is understood in the very origin that the
"Thou" of the mother is not the "I" of the
child, but both centers move in the same ellipse
of love, and because it is understood likewise in
the very origin that this love is the highest good
and is absolutely sufficient and that, a priori,
nothing higher can be awaited beyond this,
so that the fullness of reality is in principle
enclosed in this "I"-"Thou" (as in paradise)
and that everything that may be experienced
later as disappointment, deficiency and yearning
longing is only descended from this: for this
reason, everything—"I" and "Thou" and the
world—is lit up from this lightning flash of
the origin with a ray so brilliant and whole
that it also includes a disclosure of God.

Explorations in Theology III:
Creator Spirit, 15

The human being who first addresses the child
is himself the recipient of his own being, so
while he does represent the Father in some sense,
he can only point in his direction.

Theo-Drama III: The Dramatis Personae:
The Person in Christ, 459n7

Balthasar draws an analogy between the way in which a
loving caregiver radiates love to a child and the way in
which God radiates love to us, enabling us to perceive
Being, and therefore God himself, as love, especially
through God's self-revelation and self-gift in Jesus Christ:

After a mother has smiled at her child for many days and weeks, she finally receives her child's smile in response. She has awakened love in the heart of her child, and as the child awakens to love, it also awakens to knowledge: the initially empty-sense impressions gather meaningfully around the core of the Thou. Knowledge (with its whole complex of intuition and concept) comes into play, because the play of love has already begun beforehand, initiated by the mother, the transcendent. God interprets himself to man as love in the same way: he radiates love, which kindles the light of love in the heart of man, and it is precisely this light that allows man to perceive this, the absolute Love: "For it is the God who said, 'Let light shine out of darkness', who has shone in our hearts to give the light of the knowledge of the glory of God in the face of Christ" (2 Cor 4:6). In this face, the primal foundation of being smiles at us as a mother and as a father. Insofar as we are his creatures, the seed of love lies dormant within us as the image of God (*imago*). But just as no child can be awakened to love without being loved, so too no human heart can come to an understanding of God without the free gift of his grace—in the image of his Son.

Love Alone Is Credible, 76

One can also say that God, who inclined toward his new-born creature with infinite personal love, in order to inspire him with it and to awaken the response to it in him, does in the divine supernatural order something similar to

a mother. Out of the strength of her own heart
she awakens love in her child in true creative
activity. Of course, God is not man, and his
inclining in grace is therefore something different
than when one human heart turns lovingly to
another. Nevertheless, the analogy is of some
value, particularly if the love of the mother is
a pure unselfish love and, hence, draws on the
power of the absolute divine store of love. The
essential thing is that the child, awakened thus to
love, and already endowed by another's power
of love, awakens also to himself and to his true
freedom, which is in fact the freedom of loving
transcendence of his narrow individuality. No
man reaches the core and ground of his own
being, becoming free to himself and to all
beings, unless love shines on him.

A Theological Anthropology, 87

Two final themes that I would like to include from
Balthasar's writings on filial love: Balthasar emphasizes that
we should teach our children to be thankful to God, not
just for specific things they receive, but also for the gift of
existence itself, and that we should teach our children to
become generous, loving people who pass on the divine
gifts of life and love to others:

[The growing child] should not be taught to
be thankful only for specific things received, but
his original awareness that he himself—his
"I"—is something given and that he must give
thanks for it, should be also transposed into the
sphere of the maturing consciousness. To be a

child means to owe one's existence to another, and even in our adult life we never quite reach the point where we no longer have to give thanks for being the person we are.
Unless You Become Like This Child, 49

If someone is a believer, he will never cease being struck with amazement at the mystery of the begetting of a child. How can a purely physiological process produce a human person who is free, spiritual, enjoys an immediate relation to God—how, indeed, unless the all-begetting origin, God himself, is involved? Every man who is in any way religious will owe lifelong thanks for himself, not only to his parents, but also to God. After all, it was God who gave man his [man's] own self as the highest and primary of all worldly goods. Even if one were to insist on describing man's freedom as "autonomous" (which in a certain restricted sense is legitimate), this autonomy is still one that derives from the original treasury of God's absolute freedom. The free man will always have to relate back to *that* freedom in order to know how to use his own freedom, to break through to a higher freedom, to realize the good.
Mary: The Church at the Source, 127

The spirit of the Christian family is traced back to the fact that all its members are children of God.
Light of the Word, 266

Morally healthy and responsible parents do not procreate and bear a child primarily

for themselves, which would be a form of
egotism, but abandon themselves into the great
movement of life, which *gives itself away* to
further generations and consents when the newly
begotten child becomes independent, "leaves his
father and his mother and cleaves to his wife",
and becomes a giver of the gift in his own right.
What is begotten is one who can beget: such is
God's deepest intention in creating. He always
entrusts something of his creative power to the
responsibility of his creature.... He must show
that he has understood God's gesture of gift-
giving by taking it over and becoming a giver: not
only in the generation of children, but in every
kind of human communication and fruitfulness.
Mary: The Church at the Source, 128–29 (italics added)

11

Self-Love as Self-Giving

Because Balthasar places such strong emphasis on various aspects of *selflessness* in love, one might conclude that he rejects self-love entirely. Such is not the case, however, as the following passages show (note especially that Balthasar states that love of God does not abolish love of self):

> I only appreciate fully that God is my
> "highest good" when I learn (in the Son)
> that I am a "good" to him, affirmed by him;
> this is what guarantees my being and my
> freedom. And it is only when I learn that I
> represent a "good" and a "thou" to God that
> I can fully trust in the imparted gift of being
> and freedom and so, affirmed from and by
> eternity, really affirm myself too.
>
> *Theo-Drama II: The Dramatis Personae: Man in God*, 287

> Perfect (intuitive) self-awareness would be an
> awareness of one's own origin from God and thus
> an indirect intuition of God. Perfect love of self
> would be a love of this origin from God, of this
> gift-quality of one's own being; perfect self-love
> would thus be indirect love of God. The deeper,

> therefore, one's love of self, the closer it is
> to the love of God, *which does not abolish the*
> *former.* This is said ontologically speaking, without
> prejudice to a practical education in the love
> of God, which naturally cannot be attained
> through introversion but only through the
> "leap out of oneself".
> *The Grain of Wheat*, 6 (italics added)

> [One should strive] to love oneself in God, as a
> gift bequeathed to us by him. To love oneself
> with the same reverence—and to help build up
> and beautify the temple of the Holy Spirit in us
> with the same painstaking devotion—as we would
> employ in any other act of divine service.
> *The Grain of Wheat*, 96

Thus, it is good to love ourselves as created and affirmed as good by God and as a gift given to us by God. However, the deepest way of loving ourselves is by loving God and God's gift of self (and hence the divine life) offered to us in God's Word, Jesus Christ:

> The created "I" loves and affirms itself at the
> deepest level by loving God's absolute, free
> "I" that manifests itself to him in the Word;
> by receiving the word of God, not as an alien,
> heteronomous truth standing over against him,
> but as his very own, his innermost truth.
> *Prayer*, 23–24

Jesus reveals our "innermost truth" to us, i.e., that we were created by God out of love so that we might share in

the divine life of love forever. Jesus has revealed the nature
of divine love as self-gift, and thus self-gift is the norm for
all of our loves: love of God, love of neighbor, *and* love
of self:

> [Jesus] provides for us in himself the divine
> norm, which in turn must be our norm. Self-love
> now can only be expressed as self-giving.
> *You Have Words of Eternal Life,* 158

Paradoxically, then, the best way to love oneself is not to
turn inward and focus on the selfish pursuit of the fulfillment of one's own wants and desires ("being for oneself"),
but rather to step out of oneself in self-giving love toward
God and neighbor ("being for others"), for it is by doing
so that we join in the fullness of God's own life:

> By bursting his boundaries in "being for",
> [man] gains a share in the fullness of divine
> and cosmic being, being that comes from
> the center of the One who is at once
> both God and man [Jesus Christ].
> *You Have Words of Eternal Life,* 90

Part IV

The Rewards of Love

After hearing Balthasar speak so much of the selflessness and sacrifice that genuine love requires, many people today are likely to ask the same question: "What's in it for me?" (to put it in its most crass form). In other words, is love *only* about self-sacrifice and suffering on behalf of God and neighbor? Are the "fruits" of love only for the beloved and not the lover? Ultimately, Balthasar's answer to the latter two questions is a definite "No", and his answer to the question of "What's in it for me?" is "More than you could ever have hoped for or imagined." At the most fundamental level, Balthasar reminds us that we are called to open ourselves up not only to *give* love, but also to *receive* the gift of love; as such, we are the beneficiaries of others' love: of God's love first and foremost, but also of the people in our lives who love us directly (should we be so blessed) and of the countless people in the communion of saints whose "spiritual goods" grace our lives without our even knowing (in this earthly life, anyway) the source of those graces.

Sure, most of us are quite willing to be the *recipients* of others' love (although for some of us, even this is difficult, often due either to an excessive pride that desires total self-sufficiency and therefore refuses to accept the gift of love from anyone, or to an excessive self-deprecation that judges oneself to be unworthy of love). But what about the more challenging part of our divine call, the call to *donative* love?

What's in *that* for us? Balthasar acknowledges that donative love "does not exclude the thought of being rewarded", but he also insists that the desire for a "reward" is not the primary focus of genuinely donative love:

> *L'amour pur* [pure love] does not exclude the
> thought of being rewarded. Love rejoices over
> the "reward" and the prospect of being united
> forever with the beloved. But love is not based
> on reward as a necessary condition.
> *The Grain of Wheat*, 88

If donative love desires a "reward", Balthasar says that it is only to be loved in return:

> Love desires no recompense other
> than to be loved in return.
> *Love Alone Is Credible*, 107

Ideally, love, as the essence of God and hence the essence of the ultimate good, is to be engaged in for its own sake:

> If love, as such, is genuine, it has
> no other ground but itself.
> *Theo-Logic III: The Spirit of Truth*, 441

> Love is always for nothing. Love has no purpose
> beyond itself and has no reward beyond itself.
> *You Have Words of Eternal Life*, 106

> Just think of the relationship between lovers: if he
> himself loves, the beloved does not take in order
> to have, in order to become rich, but because it
> is the lover's joy to give. But the lover himself

would like to enrich the beloved through his
gift: he does not give in order himself to enjoy
the giving of it. Therefore, in order to gratify the
lover (in order to give his gift back to him), the
receiver accepts it in such a way that he really
finds himself enriched and shows it.
The Grain of Wheat, 87

The latter passage begins to hint at a profound truth: the
fulfillment of our deepest desires as human beings (such as
our desires for happiness, meaning, and freedom and our
desires for beauty, goodness, and truth) is found *via* love,
i.e., indirectly through a loving life, rather than via the
self-centered, direct pursuit of these other goods. Balthasar
provides a pithy expression of this truth:

Absolute fullness ... does not consist of
"having", but of "being=giving". It is
in giving that one is and has.
*The Glory of the Lord VII: Theology:
The New Covenant*, 391

Thus, one of the deepest spiritual truths turns out to be
a paradoxical one (like most spiritual truths, interestingly
enough): our ultimate fulfillment as human beings is not
found in *having* (i.e., in selfishly pursuing as many goods as
we can grab for ourselves), like most people today tend to
assume, but rather in *giving*, for it is then that we are most
fully *alive*, that we share most fully in the infinite life of
God, who *is* self-giving love.

And there is another paradoxical truth that follows
closely on the heels of this first one: if we renounce our
egocentrism, if we break out of our self-enclosed ego and

open ourselves up more fully to *giving*, we then end up *having* the goods that we had previously thought could only be obtained through egocentric pursuit: happiness, meaning, freedom, etc. *Having* lies on the far side of *giving*, but only if the giving is done without a focus on having.

12

The Only True Happiness

Many people today seem to believe that human fulfillment (and, therefore, ultimate happiness) lies in *having*,
not *giving*, and that life is, therefore, all about the pursuit
of as much stuff (money, pleasure, power, status, etc.) as
one can accumulate. Balthasar attempts to help people see
where ultimate happiness lies by framing the issue in at
least two different ways, both of which involve a choice
between finitude and infinity. We can seek to find our
ultimate happiness via the possession of finite goods or else
via possession of the infinite Good, who is God. Expressed
in another way, we can seek to find our ultimate happiness
within the confines of our finite, self-enclosed ego, or we
can transcend our ego and seek ultimate happiness within
the infinite life of God.

Balthasar approvingly cites Saint Thomas Aquinas
regarding the inability of finite goods to satisfy the infinite
desires of our hearts:

> After having shown that there are not many
> ways in which man's freedom is able to find
> complete fulfillment, and having discoursed on
> particular goods that in every case fail to bring
> fulfillment—on riches, honors, and fame (or
> posthumous reputation); on power (!), health

of body, sensual pleasure (coarse or sophisticated),
and inner quiet of soul—[Aquinas] then
shows that only the eternal God can fulfill the
longing gaze of human freedom.
Engagement with God, 67

Balthasar acknowledges the genuine *goodness* of finite
goods, but also notes their ultimate failure to satisfy us:

Who is presumptuous enough to assert that
the finite is enough for us, that a secret
happiness in some earthly nook—a few years,
a subdued happiness, a modest happiness—
is enough for the heart?
Heart of the World, 52

[To seek our ultimate fulfillment in the possession
of finite goods] would be seeking to nourish the
spirit's infinite capacity for Being, for the True
and the Good, with mere finite substance.
Theo-Drama II: The Dramatis Personae: Man in God, 241

All [finite] good things ... suffer under the
incurable contradiction that we strive to attain
them and are already weary of them beforehand.
We must reach out to them, because we do not
find sufficient provisions at home to allow us to
survive the winter—and yet, we cannot pile up a
stock of them, because they flee from us: we lose
them, or they themselves lose their brightness,
their newness, their power to attract us. They
leave behind a stale, tedious emptiness, and we
are not strengthened and refreshed as we look out

for new good things but wearied and discouraged.
Once again, we have the taste of futility in our
mouth, and we know very well that this taste
will remain with us from the next adventure,
too, and from the adventure after that.
Explorations in Theology III: Creator Spirit, 537

Within finite freedom there is an element
of infinity that we may call "indifference"
toward all finite goods, or the absolute longing
for what is always beyond our grasp.
Theo-Drama II: The Dramatis Personae: Man in God, 200

The [spiritual] quest's point of departure, then,
is the insight that none of the things that
surround us in this world can be what we seek,
because all of them are finite and transitory.
Theo-Logic II: Truth of God, 90

The creature called from the realm of nothingness
into being by God has this longing for the source
of being, the transcendent ... being of God.
A Theological Anthropology, 23

Finite goods cannot provide us with ultimate happiness,
but they do point us toward the infinite Good:

Infinite good can be detected in the finite good:
the promise of greater things, the possibility of
breaking through, an enticement so sweet that
our pulse falters for keen delight, when the
marvel—conferring a boundless bliss—suddenly
discloses itself for a few moments.
Heart of the World, 20

In some of the following passages, Balthasar makes a connection between his two ways of framing the issue of ultimate happiness: many of us mistakenly seek the infinite Good via finite goods, but hopefully we eventually realize that our ultimate happiness and our ultimate fulfillment hinge on the choice we make between egocentrism and *ekstasis*, between remaining within the finite "prison" or "dungeon" of our ego and venturing out of the ego into the infinite spaces of God in response to God's personal invitation to each one of us:

> Man feels an irrepressible yearning for the highest, lasting Good and is so strongly drawn to it that he simply must seek it, even through all finite and transitory goods. He is bound to acknowledge its overwhelming superiority over his own narrow ego, which encloses him as in a prison.
> *You Crown the Year with Your Goodness*, 169

> Man is a dynamism that points into infinity but that cannot attain the Infinite unless the Infinite comes down to meet it.... And woe to us if we fail to transcend the finite! Augustine's constant refrain [is] "transcende teipsum" [Transcend yourself].
> *Explorations in Theology V: Man Is Created*, 16

> The origin of all beings and all persons, namely, [God] the Father, draws us to him, but not to swallow us up within him: he draws us to him in order to fulfill us in him in a way that transcends our own self. He is the infinite "I": from all eternity he has wanted and chosen us and addressed us by the familiar "thou". At this word,

"thou", uttered to each one of us in
a quite distinct and personal way, the closed
doors of our dungeon burst open.
You Crown the Year with Your Goodness, 169

We remain ourselves and do not become
God, and yet we become ourselves only
beyond ourselves in God.
Explorations in Theology III: Creator Spirit, 507

The creature, seeing and hearing God,
experiences the highest bliss of self-fulfillment,
but it is fulfilled by something infinitely
greater than itself, and its fulfillment and
bliss are commensurately great.
Prayer, 25

Balthasar sometimes uses the language of "possessing"
God, the infinite Good, in order to contrast that state with
the possession of finite goods, but his preference is to refer
to a "participation" or a "sharing" in the divine life via
self-emptying, self-giving love, rather than to "possessing"
God. If one insists on using the language of "possession",
Balthasar notes that such "possession" takes on a paradoxical form: one "possesses" the divine life only by giving it
away, i.e., by sharing the divine life and love with others:

[Man] could be fulfilled ... only in the possession
of the absolute Good, whom we call God.
Explorations in Theology III: Creator Spirit, 138

It is ... not possible to take God to oneself
through an act of appropriating him, because
God is personified handing-over, and one

"knows" him and "possesses" him only when one
is oneself expropriated and handed over.
The Glory of the Lord VII: Theology:
The New Covenant, 400

True *eros*, ... yearning of the heart [for God],
already bears the mark of God's kenosis. Since this
love is a yearning, its true nature is not a will to
possession but a will to self-emptying. Otherwise,
man would not be God's image and likeness.
Explorations in Theology V:
Man Is Created, 36

With respect to God there can be no will-to-
possession, since God himself has no desire to
possess. Does he not give his Son away to all,
irrevocably? Only in this way does he have him.
The Threefold Garland, 63

[Jesus speaking:] For my grace is always fruitful,
and my gift it is for you to pass my grace on.
My treasure is to be found in prodigality, and
only he possesses me who gives me away.
Heart of the World, 83

The creature's yearning [for God] cannot be
a will to power that would seize possession
of God but rather a will to surrender, to let
oneself be seized by him. And as such, it is
stamped with God's way of loving: receptivity
for his condescending love and the will to imitate
this movement of condescension in one's own
love—for God as well as for others.
Christian Meditation, 93

All of which brings us back to the spiritual truth with which we ended the introduction to this part of the book: "absolute fullness" (i.e., our ultimate fulfillment and happiness) consists in giving, not having. We truly "possess" something only if we are able to give it away. We "possess" God only by being able to pass the divine love on to others, and we "possess" our real selves only by giving and receiving the gift of self within the eternal circulation of love that constitutes both the divine life and the divine bliss and, hence, *our* ultimate bliss as well:

> From the point of view of finitude, one might suppose that the infinite self-possession of infinite reality [by God] would be bound to be the ultimate satisfaction and blessedness. But in God's self-proclamation in Jesus Christ the more blessed mystery is revealed, namely, that love—self-surrender—is part of this bliss of absolute freedom. Humanly speaking, (along with Ferdinand Ulrich), what we have here is the identity of "having" and "giving", of wealth and poverty.
>
> *Theo-Drama II: The Dramatis Personae:*
> *Man in God, 256–57*

> According to Christian Faith, self-giving constitutes the eternal blessedness of this God. Insofar as he is the primal source of everything, "Father", he gives his all, from all eternity, to his Son, and the absolute bliss of both of them is to give themselves to each other in return in the Holy Spirit, who is God as pure gift.
>
> *You Crown the Year with Your Goodness, 28*

God's entire wealth consists in this giving of
self and receiving of the "Thou".
You Crown the Year with Your Goodness, 231

Our wealth is this: to receive [Christ's]
self-giving and to respond to it by
handing it on. A process of love.
You Crown the Year with Your Goodness, 293

The fullness of blessedness lies in both giving
and receiving both the gift and the giver.
Theo-Drama II: The Dramatis Personae: Man in God, 258

Nothing can surpass the joy of exchange
and reciprocal sharing.
Theo-Logic I: Truth of the World, 45

The blessedness is found right in the sacrifice.
Light of the Word, 278

Man was not created to become resigned but
to die to himself and, having become Christ's
possession, to possess all things with him.
The Grain of Wheat, 17

[Selfless love] demands a very great deal: namely,
to subordinate everything to the love which
does not seek its own; but it gives a great deal
more: namely, the only true happiness.
Elucidations, 231

You will experience the anguish of the creature
that must humble and lose itself, but also the sheer
joy of the divine life, which consists in being a
closed circuit of endlessly flowing love.
Heart of the World, 213

Surely this circulation of life and love will not come to a halt in heaven; rather, it is there that it will reach genuine efficacy. If heaven is being in God, and if the triune God is an endless exchange among the persons of God the Father, God the Son and God the Holy Spirit, then God will draw his perfected creation into this flow of divine life. At that time, as the Lord of the Apocalypse says, each one shall receive a new name "which no one knows" except God and himself. Each one will finally know who he is in reality, and consequently each will at this time be able to make of himself a fully authentic and unique gift. And this self-giving will be common to all, so that we will not only plunge eternally into God's ever newer depths, but also into the inexhaustible depths of our fellow creatures, both angels and men.

The Threefold Garland, 137–38

13

The Meaning of the World Is Love

This yearning for the absolute is at the very
heart of man; it is the source of his search
for meaning as such, including the meaning
that he tries to discern in horizontal history.
However, none of the passing moments of
the world of time can encapsulate that desired
absolute meaning—not even that moment,
projected into an ever-receding future, when
"positive humanism" will have been attained;
on the other hand, man rejects that revelation
and *incarnation* of absolute meaning that is
manifested in terms of finite history.
Theo-Drama IV: The Action, 73

The meaning of being consists in love.
Theo-Logic I: Truth of the World, 111

We human beings search for some sort of meaning or purpose in life. What is life all about? Is there any ultimate
meaning to life, to our existence, to the existence of the
cosmos? Since at least the time of the Enlightenment and
the ascendancy of such world views as positivism, many
people have sought such meaning exclusively within their

finite, transitory lives, denying the possibility of some transcendent realm or reality that could give a deeper, more
lasting meaning to human existence. Such world views
cannot provide us with an ultimate or absolute meaning
for our lives:

> The positivism that has asserted itself
> increasingly since the Enlightenment ...
> systematically robs the individual and
> society of every horizon of meaning.
> *Theo-Drama III: The Dramatis Personae:*
> *The Person in Christ*, 460

> All this profane existence which shouts so loudly
> the importance and purposefulness of its own
> claims is ultimately meaningless, for it cannot find
> in its own realm any ultimate grounding; it retains
> something of a ghostly and despairing character,
> it flees from one meaningless present into an
> ostensibly more meaningful future, a future
> however whose deep perilousness, ambiguity,
> unredeemability, is an open secret for all.
> *Elucidations*, 188

Thus, Balthasar speaks of [modern man's] bankruptcy in the
face of the question of ultimate meaning (*Theo-Drama II:
The Dramatis Personae: Man in God*, 125).

As with his discussion of human happiness, Balthasar
frames his discussion of meaning in terms of a dichotomy
between finite meaning and infinite, "absolute", or "ultimate" meaning. He does acknowledge that our finite,
transitory lives can yield *some* meaning: loving relationships formed and maintained, accomplishments achieved
in one's work, etc. However, the meaning these can

provide is *finite* and therefore unable to satisfy our deepest longings for meaning. Our mortality, our finitude, is one of the major obstacles to finding such ultimate meaning or "completeness" in our lives:

> Death, it would appear, is the great rock
> thrown across the path of all thinking
> which might lead to completeness.
> *A Theological Anthropology*, 48

Only an "enduring good", an infinite good, (God) could provide ultimate meaning to our lives:

> A man's existence becomes meaningful precisely
> by its direction toward an enduring good that
> makes sense of his whole life story and so
> enables him to accept both the non-sense he
> meets every day and the (apparent) absurdity
> of the world itself ... [— a] reorientation
> of existence toward ultimate meaning.
> *Explorations in Theology V: Man Is Created*, 272

Furthermore, we would need God to disclose to us the ultimate meaning of life; we cannot discover that meaning on our own:

> It is only God's free self-disclosure that
> can produce the key to the riddle of
> why there is a world at all.
> *Truth Is Symphonic*, 55

Of course, this is precisely what the Christian faith asserts that God has done through Jesus Christ:

God's self-giving in Christ is the
purpose of creation.
Theo-Drama IV: The Action, 62

The triune mystery of God [as self-giving love]
was impressed upon his entire creation from the
beginning.... [A]ll creatures carry a trace of this
eternal self-giving and fruitfulness. Christ and the
Holy Spirit whom he sends are not merely the
revelation of a totally new, alien mystery, but
are indeed the revelation to the creature of
his own ultimate meaning and being.
Light of the Word, 312–13

It is only "in Christ" that things can attain
their ultimate goal and meaning.
Prayer, 64

The raising of Jesus from the dead to
eternal, divine life is God's last word
on the meaning of life and death.
*Theo-Drama III: The Dramatis Personae:
The Person in Christ*, 17

Indeed, the cosmos would have no ultimate meaning
without Jesus Christ:

[Jesus] is causing the whole world to mature
into its full shape like a vast body, so that it may
attain its goal in God, that is, to exist in the fire of
eternal love of Father, Son and Spirit. If the world
did not have this goal, to be attained through the
Ascension of Jesus Christ, we should have to say
that it had no ultimate meaning. There could be

meaningful moments in the life of the individual
and in the history of mankind, but they would be
merely islands within an ocean of meaninglessness.
Atheism, of course, endeavors to construct a
total meaning in the process of world history
toward a better future. But this is bound to shatter
hopelessly when confronted with the meaningless
suffering of the countless people who die along
the utopian road without contributing the least
spark of meaning toward the process.

You Crown the Year with Your Goodness, 127

This Word of God [Jesus] descends into time
and then, in Resurrection, arises out of time,
and by doing so expresses the meaning of all
time. Only within this Word do heaven and
earth and the whole of world history acquire a
genuine meaning. In the absence of this Word,
heaven and earth are stray comets coming from
nowhere and going nowhere, lacking all sense and
purpose. It is a source of astonishment that people
who reject the all-embracing meaning to be
found in Christ or do not even know it still think
they can find a meaning in existence. In pre-
Christian times it was possible to do this to some
extent, since all peoples believed in some divinity
or other; but how could this be possible in the
post-Christian era? For there is no going back
to the more childlike world models of ancient
civilizations. Heaven and earth are empty, the
moon is a heap of stones, man is alone in
this barren waste and all will pass away.

You Crown the Year with Your Goodness, 234

We can have a rough idea of the path that
lies ahead of us in world history—namely, the
path of technology, of concentrations of
power, of the use of violence—even simply in
order to survive. Mankind will with difficulty
learn to avoid doing things it can do, for it is
made up of too many heads. And since, outside
the path of Jesus Christ, history's paths will
seem to be increasingly meaningless (whatever
man tries to do), there will be more and more
explosions of this sense of meaninglessness.

You Crown the Year with Your Goodness, 235

What are the alternatives, as Balthasar sees them?

We can take flight from the meaninglessness
of the present and put all our efforts into the
future, working for a more just distribution
of goods; but will this make people happier?
Or, like the Oriental religious man, we can try
to escape from the senseless, endless turning of
the world's wheel; but what kind of meaning
does this leave the world? All that remains is the
third possibility, the way of Jesus Christ.

You Crown the Year with Your Goodness, 236

Hope would not exist if it did not come from
the immense fire at the heart of things, if eternal
love—contrary to appearances—were not the
meaning of life. The Christian, together with
everyone who has genuine hope, fights his
way through the meaninglessness of the world.
He establishes cells and islands of conspiracy,

networks of hope in the kingdom of the dark
lord of the world. Right from the beginning
Christianity was seen as a total, highly dangerous
revolution. Why else was it so persecuted? It
is meaning's revolt against the meaninglessness
of dying, which casts a shadow of absurdity
on all that lives. It is the revolt of Resurrection
against the finality of bodily disintegration.
The revolt of love's absoluteness against any
resignation on the part of the heart.
You Crown the Year with Your Goodness, 97

The thing we call Christian hope is not
interruption but the infinite deepening and
intensification of that obscure hope of the
individual that his earthly existence has not been
totally meaningless and in vain. The individual
wants to have contributed to the building up
of the human kingdom; the Christian wants
to have contributed a little to the Kingdom of
God in the earthly and human realm.
Who Is a Christian?, 121

The eternal circulation of self-giving love within the
Trinitarian life of God *is* the ultimate meaning of life;
all human beings are invited to participate in that eternal love and thereby in the infinite meaningfulness of
the divine life. But every individual human being is also
called to a specific *mission of love* within Jesus Christ's
overall mission of love, a mission that is unique to him,
which no one else can fulfill in his place, and that therefore gives each person's life a meaning and purpose that
is also unique to him:

Through [Jesus—"Yeshua"] and in him, God's
past, present and future plan for humanity as a
whole and for each individual member of it will
be revealed—so much so that none of us will be
able to find the abiding meaning of his existence,
his ultimate relationship with God, apart from
this Yeshua. He is God's personal address to all,
and hence his personal address to me.

You Crown the Year with Your Goodness, 295–96

The Christian, in his personal as in his social
life, is not truly himself until he is within God's
involvement in Jesus, by which he is rescued
from his state of alienation where his
"understanding lay darkened", and, being
delivered from the "power of darkness", is
brought into the clear light of self-knowledge
that reveals to him his true identity, shows
him his true vocation, and enlightens him
as to the real meaning of his existence.

Engagement with God, 28

The divine mission that each is called to
fulfill, and is entrusted with the freedom
to accomplish, makes his life meaningful,
because it communicates to him precisely the
fullness that his innate creaturely capacities could
never have enabled him to attain on his own.

Explorations in Theology V: Man Is Created, 385

This mission can be anything: a mission of prayer,
of suffering, of active involvement for the poor
and oppressed, a mission to a small circle of people

who need support and the comfort of a light, a
public mission or a hidden mission, a successful
mission or one doomed to failure: the only
important thing is that man stays faithful to it.
You Crown the Year with Your Goodness, 205

[E]ach of us has an assigned task.... No matter
what we are doing, whether spiritual or secular,
we are doing [it] for [God], not for ourselves. We
are building his Kingdom, not our own.
Light of the Word, 149

In the kingdom of God there are no mere
spectators; each person has some task or other.
And there is a fluid spectrum from the great,
attested missions that the Church sets before
us as models to be imitated [those of the saints]
and the little everyday tasks that most of us have.
At [the Feast of] "All Saints" we are by no
means celebrating primarily the great and
impressive model missions but also the missions
of all who are called to holiness of whatever
kind and have reached it in whatever way.
These include all Christians of goodwill who
ultimately are not seeking their own private
happiness and salvation but are endeavoring
to serve God and their fellowmen.
You Crown the Year with Your Goodness, 208

In Christ's constant Today we live for him
and for one another. Each of us has a personal,
irreplaceable task, but not for its own sake, rather
for the living whole. Each of us has to carry out
our mission in the Spirit of the whole, the Spirit

who assigned that which is specific to each of
us. Since all of us "have been given to drink
of the one Spirit", each of us who has the
Spirit must live outside himself, in love
to the other, in the other.
Light of the Word, 273

Everyone who serves is a unique human being,
and the love in his heart is irreplaceable. He pours
his personal love into the great anonymous whole.
Who Is a Christian?, 119

And there is the remarkable thought that all of my
sparse and generally so unbelievably disappointing
action has some meaning in relation to the human
future: that in the end my vanishingly small
contribution makes a difference in the immense
sum of the whole—a difference, to be sure,
which scarcely anyone will think about after
my death, yet which nonetheless was there
and went into the reckoning, which would
not have worked out quite so easily without
me if it should ever work out at all.
Convergences, 112–13

If a person accepts his God-given mission in Christ and
carries it out (with the assistance of God's grace), that mission will yield fruit for the entire *communio sanctorum:*

[A person's mission] ... makes up the unique,
distinctive "personality" of each single
Christian and his gift, which is to be distributed
fruitfully in the communion of saints.
Life Out of Death, 88

If a mission is accepted and carried out, it de-
privatizes the "I", causing the latter's fruitful
influence (through grace) to expand into the
whole "Mystical Body" of Christ. In this way,
there is a mutual interpenetration of the diverse
missions and the persons who identify themselves
with them: this is what is meant by the *communio
sanctorum*. Evidently it is not only the goods and
values of these persons that become common
property but the persons themselves.
Theo-Drama III: The Dramatis Personae:
The Person in Christ, 349

Balthasar sums all of this up in another beautiful passage
from *Heart of the World*:

[Jesus speaking:] For in you [the Church] my
individual Heart, too, widens to become the
Heart of the World. You yourself are the holy
heart of the nations, holy because of me, but
unifying the world for me, making my Blood
circulate throughout the body of history. In you
my redemption ripens, I myself grow to my full
stature, until I, two-in-one with you, and in the
bond of the two-in-one flesh—you, my Bride and
my Body—will place at the feet of the Father the
Kingdom which we are. The bond of our love
is the meaning of the world. In it all things reach
fulfillment. For the meaning of the world is love.
Heart of the World, 202–3

14

Nothing Is as Free as Love

[There is a] cloudless horizon into which every
personal freedom yearns to sail: the
unfathomable ocean of freedom as such.
Explorations in Theology V: Man Is Created, 375

As was the case with our desire for happiness and our desire
for meaning, our desire for freedom is infinite. Therefore,
as was also the case with our desire for ultimate happiness and ultimate meaning, our desire for ultimate freedom
can only be fulfilled through participation in infinite freedom, the freedom of God. This is a key theme in Balthasar's
theology, a theme that he expressed repeatedly throughout
his writing:

Finite freedom can only fulfill itself within
the realm of infinite freedom.
Theo-Drama II: The Dramatis Personae:
Man in God, 292

Finite freedom must return to [its] source [God's
infinite freedom] in order to reach its goal (that
is, its own total liberation, which can only be
found in unconditional, infinite freedom).
Theo-Drama IV: The Action, 370

The free man will always have to relate back to
that freedom [God's freedom] in order to know
how to use his own freedom, to break through
to a higher freedom, to realize the good.
Mary: The Church at the Source, 127

The more completely man participates in God's
freedom, the freer he is, and it is only within
the realm of God's freedom that man can
realize his potentiality for freedom.
The Moment of Christian Witness, 82

There is only true freedom when we are
in contact with the Good, in the
atmosphere of love—that is, of God.
You Crown the Year with Your Goodness, 78

In the following passages, Balthasar emphasizes that in
accepting God's invitation to enter into the infinite freedom of the divine life, our finite freedom is not *absorbed
into* the infinite freedom of God but rather finds its ultimate fulfillment in a *participation in* the infinite freedom
of God. He also makes the connection that is crucial for
us in this chapter: God's infinite freedom is *identical* to his
essence as self-giving love; therefore, our finite freedom
finds its ultimate fulfillment by entering into the infinite
freedom of the divine dynamic of self-giving love:

Finite freedom is not absorbed into infinite
freedom but stays eternally itself; yet it does not
remain as a mere counterpart to infinite freedom:
it is a freedom that is fulfilled in and through the
infinite freedom, which is freely self-giving love.
Theo-Drama II: The Dramatis Personae: Man in God, 233

Freedom, in its full sense, only exists in personal
participation in absolute love.
Theo-Drama IV: The Action, 378

Simplicity and freedom (which are to be found in
love, and consist in love) grow side by side.
Prayer, 132

[The Church] points to love as
the path to freedom.
You Have Words of Eternal Life, 194

Nothing is as free as love; apart from love, all
so-called freedom is no freedom at all.
Prayer, 128

Even freedom is not superior to love; after
all, [freedom's] fulfillment consists in its placing
itself voluntarily at the disposal of love and
in losing itself in love.... Ultimately, nothing
is freer than the love that groundlessly
reveals and gives itself away.
Theo-Logic I: Truth of the World, 126

The latter two passages provide a stark contrast with the
conception of freedom held by many people today, a conception that originated at the time of the so-called Enlightenment: freedom as "total autonomy"[1] or "autarchy", as
the ability to do whatever one wants. Such a conception
of freedom leaves a person at the mercy of his egocentric desires, *enslaved* to those desires, rather than truly setting that person free. If you cling to yourself and to your

[1] Hans Urs von Balthasar, *Theo-Drama: Theological Dramatic Theory*, vol. 4,
The Action, trans. Graham Harrison (San Francisco: Ignatius Press, 1994), 444.

egocentric desires, you will remain locked within the "closed sphere of [your] ego"[2] and thus fail to fulfill your desire for infinite freedom. Paradoxically, you do not fully "possess" yourself until you freely choose to give yourself away in love:

> [God] demands that a choice be made between two freedoms—a freedom, which may take a personal or a collective form, of innerworldly self-determination (*autarkeia*—autarchy), and a freedom of self-giving in faith's obedience to the free love of God. The one who chooses self-determination will remain in the "servitude" of the world and will be alienated from God, while the one who chooses self-giving has his home with God and is a "pilgrim and stranger" (1 Pet 1:1; 2:11; Heb 11:13) and a "resident alien" (1 Pet 1:17; cf. Heb 11:9) in this world.
>
> *Glory of the Lord VII: Theology: The New Covenant*, 501

> [God the Father] is ... the origin of all freedom—... not in the sense of doing as one chooses, but in that of superior self-possession of the love which surrenders itself.
>
> *Credo*, 32

Balthasar's use of the term "surrender" here leads me to my next point: Balthasar frequently draws a connection between ultimate freedom and many of the specific aspects of love already discussed in previous chapters, including self-surrender, *ekstasis*, and kenosis. First, a few more

---

[2] Hans Urs von Balthasar, *You Crown the Year with Your Goodness*, trans. Graham Harrison (San Francisco: Ignatius Press, 1989), 169–70.

passages regarding the linkage between freedom and loving self-surrender:

> [Finite freedom] attains its realization precisely by
> surrendering itself to [infinite freedom].
> *Theo-Logic I: Truth of the World*, 9

> What [God] the Father gives is the capacity
> to be a self, freedom, and thus autonomy, but
> an autonomy which can be understood only
> as a surrender of self to the other.
> *Unless You Become Like This Child*, 44

Ultimate freedom requires that one be willing to transcend oneself, to step out of oneself, in the *ekstasis* of self-giving love:

> Infinite freedom summons finite freedom to
> go beyond itself and share in the former.
> *Theo-Drama IV: The Action*, 380

> The child, awakened thus to love [by the love
> of a parent], and already endowed by another's
> power of love, awakens also to himself and to
> his true freedom, which is in fact the freedom of
> loving transcendence of his narrow individuality.
> No man reaches the core and ground of his
> own being, becoming free to himself and
> to all beings, unless love shines on him.
> *A Theological Anthropology*, 87

> All love strives to go out of itself into the
> immeasurable spaces of freedom. It seeks
> adventure and, in so doing, forgets itself.
> *Heart of the World*, 143–44

> [Finite freedom] can only *be* itself by
> being oriented *beyond* itself, to the absolute
> good.... If created freedom chooses itself
> as the absolute good, it involves itself in a
> contradiction that will devour it.
> *Theo-Drama V: The Last Act*, 301

> Only he who escapes from the
> prison of self is free.
> *Convergences*, 131

Ultimate freedom is also intertwined with the sacrifices
and the kenosis required by love:

> Christ's "forness" ... has no other goal than to
> free men from the prison of "for self" and to
> introduce them to the shape of divine freedom.
> *You Have Words of Eternal Life*, 89

> There is no inner freedom without renunciation.
> *The Glory of the Lord VII: Theology:*
> *The New Covenant*, 534

> Love makes us free if it is selfless, and it is selfless
> if it is ready to sacrifice pleasure, advantage and
> independence for the sake of the beloved.
> *Prayer*, 128

Balthasar also links freedom to the openness required by
love:

> Finite freedom can only fulfill itself in the realm of
> infinite freedom, and not by using infinite freedom
> for its own finite aims, but by opening itself up to

the self-disclosure of infinite freedom. In Christian
terms, it must allow the love of God to work upon
it, loving it in return for its own sake.

Theo-Drama II: The Dramatis Personae: Man in God, 303

If this divine self-disclosure takes place—and in
the biblical view this is the ultimate reason why
God created the world from out of himself—
something must be added to finite freedom.
It must essentially be *summoned* by the divine
freedom; it must be called to disclose itself,
open itself, to the divine self-disclosure.

Theo-Drama IV: The Action, 165–66

No single man can attain his true freedom unless
he is borne by the power of men's openness to
one another in love; if this is true of the sphere of
the human mind, then it is naturally even truer of
the man raised to loving communion with God.

A Theological Anthropology, 88

Balthasar emphasizes another way in which freedom and
love are intimately connected with each other: love is genuine only if freely given and freely received. Thus, God
grants every human being the freedom to say Yes or No
to love:

The reason for God's choosing man lies in
his love, free and groundless. It promotes as
response the free, reciprocal love of the
chosen, because free love can only be
answered with love given freely.

Engagement with God, 20

Love cannot be forced on someone
who despises it.
You Have Words of Eternal Life, 266

God can create no creature that is free yet, at the
same time, "congealed in goodness"[;] ... instead,
it is of the essence of the gift of freedom to be
able to choose one's own highest value, thereby
realizing oneself for the very first time.
Dare We Hope "That All Men Be Saved"?, 113

[God's] almightiness consists ... in exerting
an influence on the freedom of human hearts
without overpowering them. Enticing forth from
them, through the mysterious power of grace,
their free assent to the truly good. The Church
fathers used to say that God's grace works not
through force but through "persuasion" (*suasione*),
in that it suggests the choice of the better and
gives the weak human will the strength to assent
to that out of its own conviction and strength.
Credo, 65

The call of God and of Christ does not
coerce men, rather, it gives them both
the freedom and the strength to follow
out of their own motivation.
Light of the Word, 99

A central element in the call of God to the life of love is
the invitation to accept and carry out our own personal
mission of love within Christ's overall mission of love to
the world (as we discussed in the previous chapter). In
carrying out our mission, we attain the highest freedom:

To carry out one's mission, placing oneself
entirely at its disposal, means to fulfill
oneself and thus to attain to personal
freedom and self-fulfillment.
New Elucidations, 237

This gift, [the mission] which God has eternally
chosen for us, is that for which we have been
created; in choosing God's choice, we fulfill the
idea of ourselves as it exists in God and, so, attain
the highest freedom. What God chooses for
us, though, is always a mission to follow Christ
within his Church.... Only when we identify
ourselves with our mission do we become persons
in the deepest, theological sense of the word.
Explorations in Theology V: Man Is Created, 40–41

Here, Balthasar points out yet another spiritual paradox:
it is only in loving *service* to God and neighbor, including
the fulfillment of our personal mission of love, that we find
our deepest *freedom*:

By being servants of our mission, we enjoy
a freedom that is boundless.
*Theo-Drama III: The Dramatis Personae:
The Person in Christ, 266*

It is in the living out of this paradox of
freedom and service that man comes
to be most truly himself.
Engagement with God, 29

In other passages, Balthasar expresses this spiritual paradox
in terms of the connection between increasing *obedience* to
God's will (which is "always love") and increasing *freedom*:

Carrying out the divine will is always liberating
for people, no matter how difficult the situation.
The second thing is learned from Christ: God's
will is always love, and one thus always seeks
God's will in concrete instances by orienting
oneself toward the greater love.
You Have Words of Eternal Life, 18

The freedom of Christ is constantly to do the
will of the Father. To follow him in that makes
one "truly free" (Jn 8:31–32). The freedom
to which Christ calls us is his own. In that
freedom we receive a share in God's inner,
trinitarian, absolute freedom.
Light of the Word, 328

The more obedient we are to the free
Spirit of Christ, the freer and more mature
we may consider ourselves to be.
Who Is a Christian?, 92

Using our finite freedom to choose God and his will
(which is, again, always love) leads to absolute freedom,
rapturous joy, and eternal life:

Choice of the beloved and of his will, choice
out of pure, unconditional love in the frankest,
most boundless *yes* (2 Cor 1:18–20), is, when
the beloved is God, elevation to absolute
freedom.... And all is rapturously crowned when
this choice can be the answer to having been
already chosen oneself in love; then the mutual
sinking into each other becomes itself eternity.
A Theological Anthropology, 36–37

Part V

The Source of Beauty, Goodness, and Truth

Balthasar's theological masterpiece, his trilogy in fifteen volumes, is structured around three of what are known as the "transcendental" aspects of being: beauty (which he sometimes refers to as "glory"), goodness, and truth.[1] These are called "transcendentals" because "they surpass [or transcend] all the limits of essences and are co-extensive with [or permeate all] Being."[2] Balthasar chose to focus on these transcendentals because they "seem to give the most fitting access to the mysteries of Christian theology".[3] According to Balthasar, all of those mysteries ultimately revolve around love; therefore, Balthasar frequently discusses these transcendentals from the standpoint of their connections to, and their origins from, love.

---

[1] As published in English by Ignatius Press, Balthasar's discussion of beauty consists of seven volumes (*The Glory of the Lord: A Theological Aesthetics* [San Francisco: Ignatius Press, 1984–2009]), goodness, of five volumes (*Theo-Drama: Theological Dramatic Theory*, trans. Graham Harrison [San Francisco: Ignatius Press, 1988–1998]), and truth, of three volumes (*Theo-Logic: Theological Logical Theory* [San Francisco: Ignatius Press, 2000–2005]). Balthasar later wrote a summary of his trilogy in one volume (*Epilogue*) that is sometimes numbered among the volumes of the trilogy and sometimes not.

[2] Hans Urs von Balthasar, *My Work: In Retrospect* (San Francisco: Ignatius Press, 1993), 115. See also Hans Urs von Balthasar, *Epilogue*, trans. Edward T. Oakes (San Francisco: Ignatius Press, 2004), 46.

[3] Balthasar, *Epilogue*, 46.

In the following passage, we begin to get an idea of how Balthasar will define these three transcendentals:

> As the transcendentals run through all Being,
> they must be interior to each other: that which
> is truly true is also truly good and beautiful
> and one. A being *appears*, it has an epiphany: in
> that it is beautiful and makes us marvel.
> In appearing it *gives* itself, it delivers itself to
> us: it is good. And in giving itself up, it *speaks*
> itself, it unveils itself: it is true (in itself, but
> in the other to which it reveals itself).[4]
> *My Work: In Retrospect*, 116

Beauty, then, refers to the way in which being "shows itself" to us, goodness to the way in which being "gives itself" to us, and truth to the way in which being "speaks itself" or expresses itself to us. To make this more concrete, take the example of a flower: by being accessible to our senses, the flower "shows itself" to us; by being available for us to use and enjoy (such as by cutting several flowers and placing them in a vase to decorate a room), the flower "gives itself" to us; and by being accessible to our intellects (i.e., we can examine the flower, analyze its structure and functioning, etc.), the flower "expresses itself" to our minds. Amazingly, *everything that exists* shows itself, gives itself, and expresses itself to us. Everything that exists *gives itself to us*. Self-gift is woven into the very structure of being itself. *Love* is woven into the very structure of being itself.

---

[4] The reader will note that Balthasar mentions a fourth transcendental here, that of "oneness" or "unity", but he does not choose to emphasize this transcendental in his theology.

The way in which all being "gives itself" through its beauty, its goodness, and its truth has its origins in the source of all being, God, who *is* self-gift and who *is* beauty, goodness, and truth:

> The triune mystery of God was impressed
> upon his entire creation from the beginning....
> All creatures carry a trace of this eternal
> self-giving and fruitfulness.
> *Light of the Word*, 312

> God's nature, theologically speaking, shows
> itself to be "absolute love" ... by giving itself
> away and allowing others to be, for no other
> reason than that this (motiveless) giving is
> good and full of meaning—and hence is,
> quite simply, beautiful and glorious.
> *Theo-Drama II: The Dramatis Personae:*
> *Man in God*, 272–73

We acknowledge that God alone exists of himself, whereas all created things only exist because of his almighty will and power and have their roots in something beyond all conditions. So, too, we acknowledge that God is truth pure and simple, the epitome of all truth, and that as a result he is always right, whatever he does or allows to happen. We acknowledge that God is goodness pure and simple, the epitome of all that is good, and that, consequently, whatever he sends us, we can always love him unreservedly with wholehearted homage and surrender. We acknowledge that God is the epitome of all

> beauty, and as a result we are enraptured
> as we submit to his truth and are caught
> up in rejoicing as we serve him.
> *You Crown the Year with Your Goodness*, 32–33

Love is the *ultimate* transcendental, the transcendental that underlies all the other transcendentals, the source of all beauty, goodness, and truth:

> It is the mystery of love ... that—itself
> groundless—grounds everything else.
> *Theo-Logic III: The Spirit of Truth*, 442

15

Love's Full Reality Is Inconceivably Beautiful

Balthasar discusses beauty in the first seven volumes of his theological trilogy on beauty, goodness, and truth.[1] Beauty is the way in which being shows itself to our senses, but beauty does far more than that. Beauty also points *beyond itself* to something deeper, to the very depths of being itself:

> The form as it appears to us is beautiful only because the delight that it arouses in us is founded upon the fact that, in it, the truth and goodness of the depths of reality itself are manifested and bestowed, and this manifestation and bestowal reveal themselves to us as being something infinitely and inexhaustibly valuable and fascinating. The appearance of the form, as revelation of the depths, is an indissoluble union of two things. It is the real presence of the depths, of the whole of reality, *and* it is a real pointing beyond itself to these depths.
> *The Glory of the Lord I: Seeing the Form*, 115–16

[1] Hans Urs von Balthasar, *The Glory of the Lord: A Theological Aesthetics*, 7 vols. (San Francisco: Ignatius Press, 1984–2009).

In order to read even a form within the world,
we must see something invisible as well, and we
do in fact see it. In a flower, a certain interior
reality opens its eye and reveals something
beyond and more profound than a form which
delights us by its proportion and colour.
The Glory of the Lord I: Seeing the Form, 433

In pointing beyond itself to the depths of being, beauty
ultimately points to *God*. The beautiful object is *epiphany*
or *theophany*, a revelation of God:

Everything in the world that is fine and beautiful
is *epiphaneia* [epiphany], the radiance and
splendour which breaks forth in expressive form
from a veiled and yet mighty depth of being.
The Glory of the Lord II: Studies in Theological Style:
Clerical Styles, 11

Every worldly being is epiphanic.... This
phenomenal form of the entity is the way it
expresses itself; it is a kind of voiceless, yet not
inarticulate, speech. It is the way in which things
express not only themselves but the whole of
reality existing in them as well, a reality that, as
non subsistens, points to the subsisting real: "The
heavens are telling the glory of God."
Epilogue, 59

[The Scholastic theologians] reinforce
transcendentality of the beautiful in the
sense of a theophanic presence of the
glory of God in all being.
The Glory of the Lord IV:
The Realm of Metaphysics in Antiquity, 391

On this point, Balthasar approvingly cites the view of the Renaissance Catholic philosopher Marsilio Ficino (1433–1499), who "interpret[s] all being as beauty, for he sees in it the gracious self-radiation of the Good [as described by Plato], deepened in a Christian sense as eternal love."[2] In pointing to the depths of being, beauty points to its source, which (or, better said, Who) is love:

> [Beauty points to] the ultimate source from
> which all beauty in its appearing flows. The name
> of this source and centre is, without qualification,
> love, in its incomprehensible passing over from
> itself into what is other than itself.
> *The Glory of the Lord II: Studies in Theological Style:*
> *Clerical Styles*, 359

In this context, Balthasar also cites Saint Gregory of Nyssa (ca. 335—ca. 395) and Saint Bonaventure, both of whom refer to the God of love as "*anelpiston kallos*, 'beauty past all hope'".[3] Balthasar himself refers to God as "the epitome of all beauty".[4] In what does God's beauty/glory consist? Self-giving love:

> [God's] glory is identical with the "selflessness"
> of the reciprocal self-surrender of the divine
> hypostases [Father, Son, and Holy Spirit]; thus,

---

[2] Ibid., vol. 5, *The Realm of Metaphysics in the Modern Age*, ed. Brian McNeil, C.R.V., and John Riches, trans. Oliver Davies, Andrew Louth, Brian McNeil, C.R.V., John Saward, and Rowan Williams (San Francisco: Ignatius Press, 1991), 253.

[3] Hans Urs von Balthasar, *The Glory of the Lord*, vol. 2, *Studies in Theological Style: Clerical Styles*, ed. John Riches, trans. Andrew Louth, Francis McDonagh, and Brian McNeil (San Francisco: Ignatius Press, 1984), 352.

[4] Hans Urs von Balthasar, *You Crown the Year with Your Goodness*, trans. Graham Harrison (San Francisco: Ignatius Press, 1989), 33.

by seeing God's glory as the goal of everything
that happens, all things are opened up to
the *gratis* of love.
Theo-Drama II: The Dramatis Personae: Man in God, 88

Self-surrender displays an inherent,
irreplaceable beauty.
Epilogue, 84

Love's full reality is inconceivably glorious.
Heart of the World, 31

As the revelation of the inter-Trinitarian love, and as God's
loving gift of self to all human beings, Jesus Christ is the
ultimate icon of beauty:

The Son is the inviolable manifestation of
the Father and of his self-giving.
Theo-Drama IV: The Action, 52

What God wishes to say to man is a deed
[Jesus' Incarnation and salvific death and
Resurrection] on his behalf, a deed that
interprets itself before man and for his sake....
What we intend to say about this deed ... is
that it is credible only as love—specifically,
as God's own love, *the manifestation of which
is the glory of God* [italics added].
Love Alone Is Credible, 10

From [Jesus'] form there shines forth
God's objective glory.
The Glory of the Lord I: Seeing the Form, 198

The Son ... [is] the *eidos* or form of God and,
thus, [is] the aesthetic model of all beauty.
The Glory of the Lord I: Seeing the Form, 592

Balthasar also quotes Fyodor Dostoevsky on this point:

> "There is really only one positively
> beautiful figure: Christ."
> *The Glory of the Lord V:*
> *The Realm of Metaphysics in the Modern Age,* 190

Balthasar claims, and rightly so, that many people today have lost the ability to perceive beauty, especially the absolute beauty of Jesus Christ and hence the beauty of self-giving love. Balthasar identifies this modern blindness to beauty as one of the primary reasons that he chose to begin his theological trilogy with a focus on beauty/glory:

> Our choice to begin with "glory" is comparable
> to what was once called apologetics, or, if you
> will, fundamental theology. Our idea was that
> today's positivistic, atheistic man, who has
> become blind not only to theology but even to
> philosophy, needed to be confronted with the
> phenomenon of Christ and, therein, to learn to
> "see" again—which is to say, to experience the
> unclassifiable, total otherness of Christ as the
> outshining of God's sublimity and glory.
> *Theo-Logic I: Truth of the World,* 20

Balthasar notes that when one loses the ability (or willingness) to perceive beauty, one also tends to lose the ability to perceive the good and the true as well, in words that have turned out to be prophetic. Many people today reduce the good (as well as the beautiful) to the level of subjective judgment rather than objective reality and reduce truth to only those "facts" that can be empirically observed and measured (scientism):

Our situation today shows that beauty demands
for itself at least as much courage and decision
as do truth and goodness, and she will not allow
herself to be separated and banned from her
two sisters without taking them along with
herself in an act of mysterious vengeance.
The Glory of the Lord I: Seeing the Form, 18

In a world which is perhaps not wholly without
beauty, but which can no longer see it or reckon
with it: in such a world the good also loses its
attractiveness, the self-evidence of why it must
be carried out. Man stands before the good and
asks himself why *it* must be done and not rather
its alternative, evil. For this, too, is a possibility,
and even the more exciting one: Why not
investigate Satan's depths? In a world that no
longer has enough confidence in itself to affirm
the beautiful, the proofs of the truth have lost
their cogency. In other words, syllogisms may
still dutifully clatter away like rotary presses or
computers which infallibly spew out an exact
number of answers by the minute. But the logic
of these answers is itself a mechanism which no
longer captivates anyone. The very conclusions
are no longer conclusive. And if this is how the
transcendentals fare because one of them has been
banished, what will happen with Being itself?
The Glory of the Lord I: Seeing the Form, 19

In fact, the person who loses the ability to perceive beauty
tends eventually to lose the ability to pray and even to love:

We can be sure that whoever sneers at [beauty's]
name as if she were the ornament of a bourgeois
past—whether he admits it or not—can no longer
pray and soon will no longer be able to love.

The Glory of the Lord I: Seeing the Form, 18

So what is to be done? We must help our fellow human
beings to discover/rediscover (and to *experience*) the objec-
tivity, the reality, of the beautiful, especially the absolute
beauty of the divine self-giving love:

The beautiful, then, will only return to us if
the power of the Christian heart intervenes
so strongly between the other world salvation
of theology and the present world lost in
positivism as to experience the cosmos as the
revelation of an infinity of grace and love—not
merely to believe but to experience it.

Explorations in Theology I: The Word Made Flesh, 109

However, for anyone to be able to perceive, and truly
experience, the beautiful (and, therefore, the depths of being
to which beauty points), he has to open himself up to that
beauty:

If we lack receptivity to it, we can blindly pass
by the most magnificent work of art.

Theo-Drama II: The Dramatis Personae: Man in God, 29

Beauty retails the mystery of being on every
street corner, yet only those who have an
adequate sensibility can understand it.

Theo-Logic I: Truth of the World, 224–25

When we open ourselves up to beauty, beauty has the power to engage us and to touch us at a profound level of our being:

> Before the beautiful—no, not really *before*
> but *within* the beautiful—the whole person
> quivers. He not only "finds" the beautiful
> moving; rather, he experiences himself
> as being moved and possessed by it.
> *The Glory of the Lord I: Seeing the Form*, 240

This is the experience that God wills for us when we encounter the beauty of divine love as revealed in Jesus Christ, but the depth of that experience hinges on the extent to which we open ourselves up to the ultimate beauty of self-giving love:

> Basically, in Jesus Christ's death, Descent
> into Hell and Resurrection, only one reality
> is there to be seen: the love of the triune God
> for the world, a love which can only be
> perceived through a co-responsive love.
> *Mysterium Paschale*, 262

> The power to see the glory of love requires
> at least a seed of supernatural love.
> *Love Alone Is Credible*, 60

> "Who is able to interpret beauty aright in
> its appearing?" For [Saint] Bonaventure, only
> the pure heart can do this, the heart that
> understands the love which reveals itself through
> beauty as love and is already prepared to respond
> with love: the potential sacrifice in the heart of

the one who is addressed, touched, and
inflamed answers to the gratuitousness of the
beauty which offers itself as a gift.

*The Glory of the Lord II: Studies in Theological Style:
Clerical Styles*, 349

16

The Goodness of Being:
Being Gives Itself

The goodness of being ... consists in
self-communication.
Theo-Logic I: Truth of the World, 220

[In] divine love, and every love that reflects
it ... the pure, unmotivated nature of
goodness comes to light, as the ultimate
face, *prosōpon*, of the Divinity.
Theo-Logic III: The Spirit of Truth, 227

God is, by definition, the ultimate Good, and the essence
of God is self-giving love; hence the essence of the ultimate good consists in self-giving love. God, in his loving
freedom, created the cosmos to share in this ultimate good
of love:

The immanent Trinity must be understood
to be that eternal, absolute self-surrender
whereby God is seen to be, in himself,
absolute love; this in turn explains his
free self-giving to the world as love.
Theo-Drama IV: The Action, 323

The life of the Trinity is a circle, eternally
fulfilled in itself; it does not need the world. As
for the act of creation, it is founded on trinitarian
freedom, "selflessly" granting to needy creatures
a share in this life of blessed selflessness.
Theo-Drama III: The Dramatis Personae:
The Person in Christ, 287

Unfortunately, we human beings turned away from the
divine love, which is one of the ways in which "sin" can
be defined: to sin is to turn away from love or reject love.
To reject love is to reject the good, since love is the essence
of the highest good.

Whatever else sin is, it is lack of love.
Elucidations, 254

Sin alone gives man the mentality of the
private individual, because it deprives him ...
of the spirit of communion and of the will
to selfless communication [i.e., love].
Mary: The Church at the Source, 110

The sinner estranges himself from, and turns
his back on, God [who is absolute love] by
his own decision, so that it is not God who
rejects him but he who rejects God.
Explorations in Theology V:
Man Is Created, 248–49

God is not only infinite freedom but also, above
all, infinite love. Sin is primarily an offense against
the latter; it is a turning away from it and a falling
from love's sphere. The sinner cannot of his own

volition return to this sphere: he needs the free
initiative of divine love if he is to do so.
Theo-Drama IV: The Action, 378

God could have left us turned away from the divine love,
but God instead took drastic action: God reconciled the
world to himself through Jesus Christ. This *action* of God,
this active involvement in the world through Jesus Christ,
is the focus of Balthasar's extended discussion of "the
good" in *Theo-Drama*, which constitutes the middle por-
tion of his trilogy on the beautiful, the good, and the true:

There is nothing ambiguous about what God does
for man: it is simply *good*. Theo-drama
is concerned with the good. What God has
done is to work salvation, to reconcile the
world to himself in Christ (2 Cor 5:19); he has
taken this initiative out of love, which simply
seeks to give itself. The good has its center of
gravity neither in the perceiving nor in the
uttering: the perception may be *beautiful* and the
utterance *true*, but only the act can be *good*. Here,
in the act, there is a real giving, originating in
the personal freedom of the giver and designed
for the personal benefit of the recipient.
Theo-Drama I: Prolegomena, 18

What is taken away from sinful man through the
surrender of the Son of God is nothing other
than his alienation from the Good; what is given
to him is nothing other than inner access to
the Good, that is, true freedom. He is liberated
both toward himself and toward God.
You Crown the Year with Your Goodness, 78

What is the nature of this deed that God has performed for us in Jesus Christ? Jesus, via his Incarnation and his Passion (suffering, death, Resurrection, and Ascension into heaven), makes it possible for all human beings (in fact, all of creation) to participate in the divine life of self-giving love. In his Incarnation, in taking on human flesh and thereby uniting the divine nature with human nature in his one Person, Jesus Christ began the process of incorporating human beings and all of creation into the life of God, a process that would culminate in, and be completed by, his Passion. This process of bringing us into the divine life, of making humans divine (!), has been referred to by theologians by various names, including apotheosis, deification, divinization, theosis, and incorporation into Christ. Although Balthasar sometimes uses these terms, he prefers to use terms such as *Einbergung* (a German term that could be translated as "sheltering ingathering" or "bringing into safe harbor") or *Heimkehr* (a German term for "homecoming").[1] Balthasar knows that our fallen human nature tends toward false pride, and he is concerned that using terms such as deification and divinization may lead some people to conclude that these terms are referring to a process by which we actually *become God*. We do not; the creature cannot become God, as Balthasar himself emphasizes repeatedly.[2] God is infinite, but we are not; God is the

[1] Aidan Nichols, O.P., *No Bloodless Myth: A Guide through Balthasar's Dramatics* (Washington, D.C.: Catholic University of America Press, 2000), 224. See also Aidan Nichols, O.P., *Say It Is Pentecost: A Guide through Balthasar's Logic* (Washington, D.C.: Catholic University of America Press, 2001), 191.

[2] See, for example, Hans Urs von Balthasar, "The Fathers, the Scholastics, and Ourselves", *Communio: International Catholic Review* XXIV (2) (1997): 354, 361, 366; Hans Urs von Balthasar, *Credo: Meditations on the Apostles' Creed*, trans. David Kipp (San Francisco: Ignatius Press, 1990), 38; Hans Urs von Balthasar, *Explorations in Theology*, vol. 3, *Creator Spirit*, trans. Brian McNeil, C.R.V. (San Francisco: Ignatius Press, 1993), 507; Hans Urs von Balthasar, *Christian Meditation*, trans. Sister Mary Theresilde Skerry (San Francisco: Ignatius Press, 1989),

source of his own existence, but we are not. For these and other such reasons, we cannot become God. But we can, through acceptance of God's loving offer in Jesus Christ, *share in* or *participate in* the divine life of God. In the words of Saint Peter (2 Pet 1:3–4), we can become "partakers of the divine nature"!

As we have seen, the divine nature, the essence of God, is a life of self-giving love, and we share in the divine life by joining ourselves to Christ. Christ made that possible by first joining himself to us in the Incarnation, thereby bridging the chasm that separates our human nature from the divine nature by uniting both natures in his one Person:

> He who was God becomes man, so that
> man can be taken up to God's place.
> *Theo-Drama IV: The Action*, 244

> All of mankind has been shown the exact
> place at which and from which alone
> its old longing for *apotheosis* can
> be fulfilled[:] Christ.
> "The Fathers, the Scholastics, and Ourselves", 357

> If the impossible happens; if the absolute not
> only irradiates finitude but actually *becomes*
> finite, something unimaginable happens to
> existence: what is finite, as such, is drawn
> into what is ultimate and eternal.
> *Theo-Drama IV: The Action*, 132

57–58; Hans Urs von Balthasar, *Light of the Word: Brief Reflections on the Sunday Readings*, trans. Dennis D. Martin (San Francisco: Ignatius Press, 1983), 34; and Hans Urs von Balthasar, *You Have Words of Eternal Life: Scripture Meditations*, trans. Dennis Martin (San Francisco: Ignatius Press, 1991), 70.

The incarnate Son ... binds together
God and man, heaven and earth.
Prayer, 43

[Jesus is] the vaulting bridge which
links one shore to the other.
Prayer, 207

In the Son, therefore, heaven is open to
the world. He has opened the way from
the one to the other and made exchange
between the two possible, first and foremost
through his Incarnation (Jn 1:51).
Prayer, 52

He did not do this for his own sake ... but for
the sake of his creature, in order to give him
sanctuary and a home with him, to lend an
abiding, eternal, divine meaning to the
creature's transitory existence.
Prayer, 203

Through the Incarnation of the Son it
[God's "inner vitality", or the dynamism of
the loving exchange of the gift of self among
the three Persons of the Trinity] not only
became known to the world but the world
came to share in it, not by being absorbed
into God but by being permitted to enter
into the eternal circuit of love in God.
Light of the Word, 89

Participation in the life of God himself ...
is a completion and perfection of something

that began in the Incarnation of the
Logos [Jesus Christ].
Theo-Drama V: The Last Act, 470

One of the key words for Balthasar in the latter passage
is "began". The Incarnation of Jesus was a necessary, but
not sufficient, step in the process of God opening up the
divine life to us. The second step was Jesus' suffering,
death, Resurrection, and Ascension into heaven on our
behalf. Balthasar cites the Church Fathers on this point:

> In the act of Incarnation, the Redeemer
> [Jesus] expresses his solidarity with all
> mankind, whose nature he shares; yet,
> according to the Fathers, it is the
> *Passion/Resurrection* (together with the
> sending of the Spirit) that achieves concrete,
> objective (and subjective) redemption.
> *Theo-Drama IV: The Action,* 247–48

One of the ways that Balthasar expresses this twofold
process is to summarize the Incarnation as the "entry
of genuine eternity into time" (Jesus bringing God to
us in visible form) and the Passion/Resurrection as the
"entry of genuine time into eternity" (Jesus bringing us
to God).[3] Jesus, in his resurrected and ascended body,
takes our human nature into the heart of the divine life
forever, thereby opening up a space for us to live within
that divine life.

---

[3] Hans Urs von Balthasar, *The Glory of the Lord,* vol. 6, *Theology: The Old
Covenant,* ed. John Riches, trans. Brian McNeil, C.R.V., and Erasmo Leiva-
Merikakis (San Francisco: Ignatius Press, 1991), 412.

It is beyond the scope of this book to go into the details of Balthasar's discussion of Jesus' Passion here,[4] but I would like to give the reader some idea of Balthasar's treatment of that topic by quoting his summary of what he sees as being the five key scriptural motifs regarding Jesus' Passion, followed by some passages that elaborate upon each of those motifs:

> The quintessence of Scripture [regarding the redemptive nature of Jesus' Passion] is found in five motifs. We must take account of all five motifs if our reflection is to be truly ecclesial. (1) The Son gives himself, through God the Father, for the world's salvation. (2) The Sinless One [Jesus] "changes places" with sinners.... (3) Man is thus set free (ransomed, redeemed, released) [from the power of evil/sin]. (4) More than this, however, he is initiated into the divine life of the Trinity. (5) Consequently, the whole process is shown to be the result of an initiative on the part of divine love.
>
> *Theo-Drama IV: The Action*, 317

> 1. The reconciliation with the world achieved by God presupposed that God's "only Son" has "*given himself up* for us all", so that, as a result, he "gives us all things" (Rom 8:32). John says the

---

[4] For the reader who would like to explore this topic in more detail, I recommend the passages in Hans Urs von Balthasar, *Theo-Drama*, vol. 4, in which Balthasar details his own soteriological theory (pp. 240–44) and summarizes/critiques other soteriological theories (pp. 244–84), as well as Balthasar's treatment of this topic throughout *Mysterium Paschale: The Mystery of Easter*, trans. Aidan Nichols, O.P. (San Francisco: Ignatius Press, 2005).

same (Jn 3:16). First and foremost, Jesus is the one whom God has "given up", "delivered up" (Mt 17:22 parr.; 20:18, 19 parr., and so forth). He *allows* himself to be handed over. But, at the heart of this obedient letting-things-happen, there is an active consent, deliberate action: "I lay down my life" (Jn 10:17) "of my own accord" ([Jn 10:]18). Thus the idea arises that he is both the (sacrificial) "Lamb" who is "given up" (Jn 1:29) and the (sacrificial) Priest who surrenders himself (Heb 2:14ff.); he is both at the same time (Heb 9:14).... The Cross is essentially a matter of the "shedding of blood" (the "life substance" of Jn 10:17ff.). This "shedding of blood" is understood as the atoning (Rom 3:25), justifying (Rom 5:9) purifying factor (1 Jn 1:7; Rev 7:14) at all levels of the New Testament.... God's final and definitive covenant with men is sealed in the self-surrender of Jesus (Mt 26:28 parr.; 1 Cor 11:25).
Theo-Drama IV: The Action, 240–41

2. He gives himself "for us" to the extent of *exchanging places with us*. Given up for us, he becomes "sin" (2 Cor 5:21) and a "curse" (Gal 3:13) so that we may "become—that is, share in—God's [covenant] righteousness" and receive "the blessing of Abraham" and the "promised Spirit". He who is rich becomes poor for our sake so that we may become rich through his poverty (2 Cor 8:9). In his body, our sin and hostility are condemned (Rom 8:3; cf. Eph 2:14). The "Lamb of God who takes away the sins of the world"

(Jn 1:29; cf. 1 Jn 3:5) ... must genuinely take
[those sins] upon himself if he is to be able to
carry them away.... On the basis of this exchange
of place, we are already "reconciled to God"
(Rom 5:18) in advance of our own consent,
"while we were yet sinners". This means that
we are ontologically "transferred" (Col 1:13) and
expropriated (1 Cor 6:19; 2 Cor 5:15; Rom 14:7),
insofar as, in the Paschal event, we have died
with Christ and are risen with him (Rom 6:3ff.;
Col 3:3; Eph 2:5).... [W]e are to let what
is true in itself be true in us and for us.

Theo-Drama IV: The Action, 241–42

The central feature of Jesus' mission is the "holy"
or "wondrous exchange" so often described
by the [Church] Fathers. "He gave his soul for
our soul, his flesh for our flesh, pouring out the
Spirit of the Father in order to achieve union
and communion between God and man"
(Irenaeus). "All men were condemned to
death; but he, the Innocent One, surrendered
his body to death for all; thus all men, being dead
through him ..., should be freed from sin and the
curse and be raised from the dead" (Athanasius).
"Just as the Word became man by taking flesh,
we men are divinized by being taken into the
flesh of the Word" (Athanasius). "The Word
became flesh so that, through the incarnate Word,
flesh should become one with God the Word"
(Hilary). For the Greek Fathers, the scope of
these words also includes the "exchange" that

takes place in the Passion: in Christ's Cross and
Resurrection, as it were, the whole of human
nature is co-crucified and co-risen (Cyril).

Theo-Drama III: The Dramatis Personae:
The Person in Christ, 237–38

3. . . . [T]he fruit of the reconciliation event
can be seen more negatively, as man being
liberated from something: from slavery to sin
(Rom 7; Jn 8:34), from the devil (Jn 8:44;
1 Jn 3:8), from the "world powers" (Gal 4:3;
Col 2:20), from the power of darkness
(Col 1:13), from the law (Rom 7:1) and from
the "law of sin and death" (Rom 8:2) and, finally,
from the "wrath to come" (1 Th 1:10).

Theo-Drama IV: The Action, 242

4. However, this loosing of bonds (Lk 13:16;
Mt 12:29) is very much more than the mere
restoration of a lost freedom. It takes place
through the Holy Spirit and imparts to us
God's Holy Spirit, who calls "Abba, Father!"
in us, assuring us that we share a fellow-sonship
with Christ vis-à-vis God the Father (Gal 4:6f.;
Rom 8:10ff.). The positive side, therefore, is
that we are *drawn into the divine, trinitarian life.*
From the highest perspective, the "redemption
through his blood, the forgiveness of sins" is
only one element within the all-embracing
divine purpose. God's purpose is to enable us,
by grace, to share in Christ's sonship (Eph 1:5ff.)
by becoming "members of his body" (1 Cor 12;
Eph 4, and so forth). The New Testament

knows nothing of any other kind of freedom
than this, which is imparted by the Holy
Spirit and lived by the power of the same
Spirit (Gal 5:13, 18ff.; cf. Jn 8:31f.).

Theo-Drama IV: The Action, 242–43

5.... [T]he entire reconciliation process is
attributed to God's merciful *love*. On the basis
of the love of the Father (Rom 8:39) and of
Christ (Rom 8:35), the Son was given up
"for us all" (Rom 8:32) by the Father. It
is God's immense love for the world that has
caused him to give up his only Son (Jn 3:16)
and thereby to reconcile the world to
himself (2 Cor 5:19; Col 1:20). He has
empowered his Son to give his life "for
his sheep" (Jn 10:15), to hand on to those
who are his the kingdom that has been
delivered to him (Lk 22:30). While this
work of redemption must have something
to do with God's covenant "righteousness"
(since it is concerned with restoring and fulfilling
the covenant, which is a two-sided reality), it
remains true that everything flows from the
primary source: God's gracious love.

Theo-Drama IV: The Action, 243

This is why Balthasar describes human existence as a theo-
drama. In Jesus, God has entered into the world in visible
form, indeed, has become one of us, in order to open up
the divine life of love to the world; it is now up to each
of us to choose whether to say Yes or No to this offer of
divine love and life:

God acts for man; man responds through decision
and deed. The history of the world and of man is
itself a great "theater of the world".

My Work: In Retrospect, 86

In his discussion of the theo-drama, Balthasar places great
emphasis on the relationship between divine freedom
(God's free decision, out of love, to create the world and
to redeem the world in Jesus Christ) and human freedom
(given to us by God as a gift that we might freely choose
whether to accept or reject the offer of the divine love and
life). For each one of us, the outcome of the play hinges
on our decision of whether to say Yes or No to self-giving
love, i.e., Yes or No to the ultimate Good, who is God:

If there is to be drama, characters must face each
other in freedom. If there is to be theo-drama, the
first presupposition is that, "beside" or "within"
the absolute divine freedom, there is some other,
nondivine, created freedom; a freedom that
shares, in a true sense, something of the autonomy
of the divine freedom, both in the decision for
God and in the decision against him.

Theo-Drama II: The Dramatis Personae: Man in God, 62–63

Anyone who penetrates into the mysteries of
God recognizes more and more that the world
as a whole is created "for nothing", that is,
out of a love that is free and has no other reason
behind it; that is precisely what gives it its
only plausible meaning. Recognizing or failing
to recognize this relationship will constitute
the core of the action in theo-drama.

Theo-Drama II: The Dramatis Personae: Man in God, 260

[God] does not decide the course of the play in advance but gives man an otherwise unheard-of freedom to decide for or against the God who has so committed himself.

Theo-Drama III: The Dramatis Personae:
The Person in Christ, 21

What New Testament revelation presents ... is nothing more or less than an admonition to the utmost seriousness of all personal decisions, an invitation to keep ever in mind the possibility of definitive conscious decision against loving self-gift and for naked egoism.

Explorations in Theology V: Man Is Created, 145

Man cannot have two ultimate goods, two final goals, at the same time. He must choose. He must arrange them according to priority, so that he is clear about which good to choose when times are hard.

Light of the Word, 95

17

Love Is Truth

Balthasar deeply laments the fact that for many people, for the last one hundred years or more, "truth" has been reduced to that which is empirically measurable and verifiable and/or mathematically provable, i.e., scientific "facts":

> It is almost taken for granted these days that one
> will not accept as true what one cannot prove
> mathematically or verify with one's own senses.
> Often modern man is not even aware that this
> comes to the same thing as a naïve, perhaps
> entirely innocent atheism, because by now
> he has absorbed into his very bloodstream the
> dogma that all truth must be provable.
> *Explorations in Theology IV: Spirit and Institution*, 338

Truth is, in fact, far richer than this constricted definition, as we shall see. According to Balthasar, part of the problem with the reduction of truth to the empirically verifiable is that it sunders the truth from the other transendentals of being. The transcendentals are inextricably interwoven with each other,[1] and if one tries to separate any of the

---

[1] Hans Urs von Balthasar, *Theo-Logic: Theological Logical Theory*, vol. 1, *Truth of the World*, trans. Adrian J. Walker (San Francisco: Ignatius Press, 2000), 216.

transcendentals from the others, one ends up losing *all* of
the transcendentals, including truth, in the process:

> The transcendentals—being, oneness,
> truth, goodness, beauty—penetrate
> each other indivisibly.
> *Test Everything: Hold Fast to What Is Good*, 83

> The "transcendental" qualities of being are so
> called because each of them holds sway over
> the totality of being. They cannot, therefore, be
> marked off from one another but indwell each
> other and make their voices heard in each other.
> *The Glory of the Lord IV:*
> *The Realm of Metaphysics in Antiquity*, 21

> One cannot speak concretely about one of
> the three [transcendentals] without drawing
> the other two into the discussion.
> *Theo-Logic I: Truth of the World*, 29

> Modern rationalism, attempting to narrow the
> range of truth to a supposedly isolable core of
> pure theory, has exiled the good and the beautiful
> from the domain of the rationally verifiable,
> relegating them to arbitrary subjectivity or to
> a world of private belief and personal taste. As a
> result, the picture of being, the unified view
> of the world, is torn to shreds, so that any real
> conversation about truth becomes impossible.
> *Theo-Logic I: Truth of the World*, 29

If truth is more than that which is accessible to our
senses and hence measurable and "verifiable", what is it?

Balthasar's starting definition is that truth is the revelation, unveiling, or disclosure of being:

> We thus have an initial description of truth
> as the unveiledness, uncoveredness, disclosedness,
> and unconcealment (*a-letheia*) of being....
> Truth consists in unveiling.
> *Theo-Logic I: Truth of the World*, 37

> To the extent that being is knowable,
> it is always already unveiled as such.
> *Theo-Logic I: Truth of the World*, 207

Balthasar's starting definition of truth can already accommodate the scientific/mathematical knowledge to which many people today wish to reduce truth: we would not have such knowledge of the physical world if existent objects did not open themselves up to (i.e., were not amenable to) our scientific and mathematical analyses. But one of Balthasar's points is that such knowledge is only one aspect of truth; he emphasizes the interactive, relational aspect of the knowing process, particularly between persons, not just the analytical aspects. Learning the "truth" about others is a dynamic, interactive process involving the voluntary disclosure of one's own being on the part of one person (the "object", in this case) and the voluntary receptivity of the other person (the "subject") to that disclosure:

> Being's opening in truth is not an arelational
> "opening in itself", but an "opening for",
> an accessibility that implies that something
> has been offered to someone.
> *Theo-Logic I: Truth of the World*, 217

> The existent object's will to disclose itself and the
> knowing subject's will to open itself in receptive
> listening are but two forms of a single self-gift
> that manifests itself in these two modes.
>
> *Theo-Logic I: Truth of the World*, 111

Here we see a reappearance of a concept that we reflected upon back in chapter 5b: the "openness" of love, which involves two movements: donative openness and receptive openness. The "object" to be known must disclose or give himself to the other in the movement of donative openness, and the subject to whom the gift of self-disclosure is offered must open himself up to the proffered gift in the movement of receptive openness. Balthasar is thus making an intimate connection between love and truth. In fact, Balthasar boldly asserts that "love *is* truth"[2] [italics added].

Upon what does Balthasar base the connection he draws between truth and love? Upon the nature of God, as *revealed* (disclosed, unveiled, etc.) by Jesus Christ and the Holy Spirit. God is the ultimate reality, Being itself, and Jesus Christ and the Holy Spirit disclose the essence of God, the essence of Being, the truth about being, *truth* itself, to be self-giving love:

> This love [the divine love] alone is, at the same
> time, the truth—"grace and truth" are one
> (Jn 1:14)—so that whoever does not let love
> take over excludes himself from the truth.
>
> *Light of the Word*, 90

[2] Hans Urs von Balthasar, *Explorations in Theology*, vol. 5, *Man Is Created*, trans. Adrian Walker (San Francisco: Ignatius Press, 2014), 327.

The truth is, not a proposition or an impersonal
fact, but the revelation of absolute love.
Theo-Logic II: Truth of God, 318

God ... is truth precisely to the extent
that he is the disclosure of the
absolute mutual gift of self.
Explorations in Theology III: Creator Spirit, 275

[Jesus] is the Way to God, and anyone
who embraces this Way has eternal life;
furthermore, anyone who lives in this
Way lives in the truth and knows it.
You Crown the Year with Your Goodness, 104

If Jesus was the "expositor" of the divine
Father (Jn 1:18), it is the "Spirit of truth"
who will initiate human beings into this truth
of Jesus, who called himself "the truth",
meaning the right exposition of God.
Theo-Logic I: Truth of the World, 18

The milieu of love between Father and Son
is opened up in the Son as a result of his self–
surrender to the world; so too the Spirit's
introduction into this milieu of love, which is
truth, is also the Spirit's self-surrender to the
person who receives his testimony.... So his
"leading into all truth" is initially something
quite different from the imparting of information;
rather, he leads us from inner participation into
inner participation [in the divine life of love,
which is the truth of being].
Theo-Logic III: The Spirit of Truth, 74

[The Holy Spirit] leads the hearts of those who do
not resist him into the truth of absolute love.
Theo-Logic III: The Spirit of Truth, 201

Of course, it is absurd to say No to truth,
which is of its essence good; but God prefers
to accept this absurdity rather than overwhelm
his creature from the outside. His astounding
masterpiece is to elicit the Yes of his free partner
from the latter's innermost freedom.
Theo-Drama I: Prolegomena, 34

In the following passages, Balthasar explicates the relationship between love and truth in more detail, noting the
inseparability of love from truth but also the primacy of
love with regard to truth:

Love is inseparable from truth.
Theo-Logic I: Truth of the World, 111

Love makes us clear-sighted; it makes us
see into the depths and into the heights.
It orders and crystallizes finite truth
around the pole of absolute truth.
Theo-Logic I: Truth of the World, 130

Because the full truth can be attained only in
love, only the lover can have the real eye for it.
He alone is ready to disclose himself truly [the
donative openness of love] and thus to bring to
completion the movement in which the truth of
being comes into existence. Moreover, he alone is
able to respond selflessly [the receptive openness
of love] when another confides in and opens up

to him, perhaps seeks his help, questions him,
or calls to him. In this way, the lover brings to
completion the movement in which the truth,
this time of knowledge, comes into existence. We
therefore have good reason for saying that truth
originates from love, that love is more original
and more comprehensive than truth. Love is the
ground that accounts for truth and enables it to
be. And yet, we cannot say that love was on the
scene before truth and that love can be conceived
without truth. For the self-disclosure of being and
knowing, whose primordial name is love, also
directly and immediately bears the name of truth.
Theo-Logic I: Truth of the World, 112

Insofar as we consider the mystery of love as
lying "behind" the truth, we have to say that
all truth is reducible to it, that truth derives
its meaning as truth from it, and that, far from
mastering and explaining it as mystery, truth
must fall silent in humility before it.
Theo-Logic I: Truth of the World, 223

The ultimate ground ... is love. To be sure,
God is eternal truth and by this truth all other
things are true and meaningful. But the very
existence of truth, of eternal truth, is grounded
in love. If the truth were ultimate in God, we
could look into its abysses with open eyes. Our
eyes might be blinded by so much light, but our
yearning for truth would have free reign. But
because love is ultimate, the seraphim cover their
faces with their wings, for the mystery of eternal

love is one whose superluminous night may
be glorified only through adoration.
Theo-Logic I: Truth of the World, 272

In Christ, love—which descends vertically and
spreads itself horizontally—is made superior to
all knowledge, even the most absolute.
The Glory of the Lord VII: Theology:
The New Covenant, 453

Only the pure heart penetrates beyond the
truth to love, because precisely in God
love is also the heart of truth.[3]
The Glory of the Lord III: Studies in Theological Style:
Lay Styles, 228

In a beautiful passage in *Theo-Logic I: Truth of the World*,
Balthasar reflects at length upon the creative power of love.
More specifically, he reflects upon the ways in which love
can help a person (typically referred to as the "object" of
love) move toward the truth, i.e., toward the object's true
self (which is God's creative idea of who that person was
intended to be) and hence toward that person's intended
destiny and ultimate fulfillment. Love enables us to see the
tremendous potential that lies in another person, to hold
up for him the image of the person he could be (and was
intended by God to be), and to help empower him to
become that person:

[The object's] primordial fulfillment ultimately
lies in God's creative idea. It is this idea that
grounds the object's true unity, for it is this idea

---

[3] Here, Balthasar is restating a point made by Blaise Pascal.

that creatively founds the object's existence....
In the creative mirror of the subject, the object
sees the image of what it is and of what it can
and is meant to be. This creative act of the
subject is no longer a mere attitude of justice
but much rather an act of *love*.
Theo-Logic I: Truth of the World, 77–78

Our homecoming to the conception God has
of us eternally is an arrival at the place from
which we originated, at the place in which
we have been eternally in our own most
intimate truth and reality.
You Have Words of Eternal Life, 86–87

In the love of the mother the child finds its
consciousness and its self. In the mother's heart
it finds the support to firm its groping, fragile
existence into a form. In the Thou, wife and
husband are told and shown who he is, who she
is, in truth. Love is creative for the fellow man;
it produces an image of him with which the
beloved would not have credited himself, and
when love is genuine and faithful it gives him
the power to come closer to this image or make
himself like it. He does not want to disappoint; he
wants to show himself grateful that someone takes
him so seriously and expects so much of him.
Convergences, 128–29

In the act of knowledge it can also be the subject's
task to assist the object in attaining its truth.
For a thing often expects the knower to know

it in a way in which it does not know itself. It
approaches the knower with a lofty idea of
what knowledge can do. It wants to be
examined with an intellectual eye that will
unveil to it its own inmost being and before
which it can stand naked without injury, just
as a patient bares himself before his doctor.

Theo-Logic I: Truth of the World, 114

This special gaze, from which the object
expects so much, leads into the inner sanctum
of knowledge. In order to describe it correctly,
we have to affirm two things at once, neither
of which must give up its place to the other:
This special gaze, which is possible only in
the loving attention of the subject, is equally
objective and idealizing. That these two qualities
can be compatible is the grand hope of the
object. It hopes to attain in the space of another
the ideality that it can never realize in itself. It
knows or guesses what it could be, what splendid
possibilities are present in it. But in order to
develop these possibilities, it needs someone who
believes in them—no, who sees them already
existing in a hidden state, where, however, they
are visible only to one who firmly holds that they
can be realized, to one, in other words, who
believes and loves. Many wait only for someone
to love them in order to become who they
always could have been from the beginning. It
may also be that the lover, with his mysterious,
creative gaze, is the first to discover in the

beloved possibilities completely unknown to their
possessor, to whom they would have appeared
incredible. The beloved is like an espalier that
cannot bear fruit until it is able to climb up on
the sticks and wires that support it.... Unless the
knower presented the ideal, the object known
would never have dreamed of aspiring to it,
or else it would have grown faint because the
attempt would have seemed too fantastic. It takes
the faith and confidence of the knower animated
by love to give the thing known faith and
confidence in the truth of the ideal held before
it. At love's bidding, the object ventures to be
what it could have been but would never have
dared to be by itself alone. On the other hand,
the lover will always consider the image that he
presents to be something objective. He knows
that the possibility he sees is truly embodied in
the beloved.... [T]he lover will always regard the
realization of the ideal as a deed of the beloved....
The beloved, on the other hand, will know that
the realization of his best potentialities is, not
his merit, but the creative work of love, which
impelled him to realize them, held before him
the mirror and the ideal image, and bestowed
the strength to attain the goal.
Theo-Logic I: Truth of the World, 114–15

This ideal reality exists nowhere else than in the
love of a subject. It is only in this space that the
ideal can unfold.... The setting up of such an
image and the gradual or speedy realization of it

have to be seen as a truly creative act, in
which the lover cooperates with the beloved
and both try to fashion reality according to
the envisaged ideality. If the result is a real,
or even just approximate, correspondence,
the object thereby attains its own truth.
Theo-Logic I: Truth of the World, 116

The lover considers the ideal image of the
beloved to be his true reality and directs his
action according to it. He keeps his eyes on
the "true" image of the beloved; he addresses
him in view of this image; he treats him as
if he were this image. Thus, he overlooks
the other, "real", imperfect image.
Theo-Logic I: Truth of the World, 116

[The lover] does see the gap [between who the
beloved currently is and who the beloved could
be], but at the same time he overlooks it. He
is not interested in the beloved's faults. And by
overlooking them like this, he overcomes them.
The lover simply lets the real, imperfect image
of the beloved sink into nonbeing.... The fact
that it is ignored, that it is not even offered the
chance to unveil itself, is a powerfully effective
contribution to the work of annihilating it. Any
being that is deprived of the right to unveiling,
that is, to truth, perishes in the long run from
want of air and light.... Thus, the obverse of
the creative proposal of the ideal image is a sort
of creative effacement of the real image. The
beloved has to rely on this double creative event

of loving knowledge. In order to attain to the
ideal that is treated as the reality, the beloved
has nothing to do but act *as if* it were already
the real thing; in order to get rid of the
reality that is to be obliterated, he has nothing
to do but to act *as if* it already no longer
existed. The beloved ought to be fully aware
of the creative event happening in the lover's
knowledge. He ought to know that the lover
has recognized the deficient reality, that in this
relation he has not glossed things over or been
naively infatuated.... Having said this, we have
made the momentous discovery that there is not
only knowledge that unveils but also knowledge
that veils, that covers. Nothing is more perverse
than the opinion that the way to tackle what
should not exist is to expose its apparent truth.
No errant person is cured of his ways by having
his attention drawn to his errors. Only when
he looks at the ideal will he be capable, if at
all, of feeling repentance for the reality.
Theo-Logic I: Truth of the World, 117–18

Balthasar asserts that psychoanalysis and many other approaches to psychotherapy have made the mistake of
focusing on the client's faults, shortcomings, etc., seeking
to expose those to the light of day and analyze them; the
better approach would be to focus on the client's *potential*, on seeing and developing the good that lies within
the client. By giving us the power to help bring another
person's ideal self into existence via love, God "allots to
the creature something of his creative power even in the
domain of truth":

This veiling knowledge is the only way to help
the beloved. The refusal to realize this is one of
the unpardonable sins of psychoanalysis and of
most of the practical schools of psychology. No
one comes to any truth through analysis alone,
however "realistic" what has been uncovered may
appear to be. By breaking down a living thing
into its parts you destroy its life. By uncovering
what the gods graciously "cover with night and
dread", you do not create suitable conditions
for life. Only when the roots of the plant are
hidden in the soil can its corolla unfold healthily.
Essential to the truth of the living thing, then,
is that a part of itself must remain veiled. And it
belongs to the truth of free, intellectual substances
that a part of themselves must be consigned to
oblivion. Not every truth ... has a claim to be
perpetuated forever. An ordered cosmos of truth
comes about only by selection and preference of
some elements: a great deal that is hidden must
be fetched out, while a great deal that is unveiled
must be returned to the state of oblivion.... God
allots to the creature something of his creative
power even in the domain of truth.... *Only in
God can one man see another as he is supposed to
be. Only in the light of God can he place before the
other the ideal image. Only in reference to God can he
encourage the other to correspond to this image* [italics
added]. If he did all of these things without
God, his fancied assistance would be nothing but
arrogance and vanity; he would presume to be
better and smarter than his neighbor; he would

require his neighbor to be bound to an ideal and
would force him into total servitude to this image.
But one finite man has neither the strength nor
the authority to lay an absolute claim on another.
Without God, this supreme achievement of
human knowledge would rather be a Promethean
act that he ought never presume to take upon
himself. *Only when you can point man to God,
when you can show credibly that the image you behold
in loving knowledge is the one that God holds in his
safekeeping—only then may you take it upon yourself
to share in the fashioning of the world* [italics added].
In order to do so, you have to have learned,
better, to have received from God the grace to
love and to contemplate men in God himself,
the original source in whom the image of
knowledge and the image of love coincide.
Theo-Logic I: Truth of the World, 118–20

Love makes the impossible possible. Its power
is so great that it simply negates the reality it
sees before it and overlooks it as if it did not even
exist. "I know", says love, "that you are
not who you appear to be." Love has glimpsed
an image of the beloved, which it does not
regard as its own construction and invention
but which it understands, at least when it is
true love and not self-delusive infatuation, as a
God-given exemplar of the beloved whom this
same God has entrusted to it. For it is given to
all things to perfect themselves through and in
one another, to become in the other what they

cannot be in themselves. Love alone can offer
this assistance, this synthesis, whose power is the
opposite of psychoanalytic unmasking.
Theo-Logic I: Truth of the World, 215–16

Embedded within Balthasar's discussion of the creative
power of love in *Theo-Logic I: Truth of the World*, we find
one of his primary definitions of love, which I have already
paraphrased as the selfless gift of self, given and received.
With this definition, Balthasar establishes an intimate connection between love and truth: truth is the self-disclosure
of being; love as self-gift is self-disclosure and hence truth.
To decline to disclose oneself to others (i.e., to conceal
oneself unduly or literally "keep to oneself") and/or to
refuse to receive the proffered self-disclosure of others is a
lack of love and, hence, a form of *untruth*:

If, therefore, genuine egoism is incapable of any
truth, genuine love, by contrast, is incapable of
any untruth. For genuine love is at the source
of truth, and when this source begins to flow
as love, it cannot help [but] generate truth.
Love is the selfless communication of what is
mine and the selfless welcoming of the other
in myself. It is thus the predetermined measure
of all truth. Self-communication is a genuine
revelation of my unique being when its ultimate
raison d'être is to give myself away [*Hingabe*]
in love for its own sake. Likewise, genuine
understanding comes from the act of receiving
others' revelation when this reception is sustained
in its turn by the loving self-giving of the object's
self-offer. To the extent that love is the very

> movement that generates truth in the first place,
> it alone holds the ultimate key to the actual
> use of truth. Love is the true measure of all
> communication and of all reception.
>
> *Theo-Logic I: Truth of the World,* 123

Balthasar contrasts the openness and willingness to disclose oneself in love with "egoistic concealment", which
is the "self-enclosure of being, and, therefore, its untruth".
He notes that "love and truth are one" in the self-surrender
[*Hingabe*] of love:

> This will to transparency in love is decidedly
> opposed to egoistic concealment, which veils
> its inner mystery for itself in order to enjoy
> it in secret without having to share it with
> another. This mystery is darkness: it is the self-
> enclosure of being and, therefore, its untruth.
> It is the refusal of the self-surrender in which
> love and truth are one; and this refusal is sin. It
> is the darkening of being in its refusal to disclose
> itself. In a loving being, there can be much
> mystery, but this mystery is light. In love, there
> is infinite depth, but no darkness. It lives in the
> attitude of wanting to keep nothing back for
> itself, of being ready to give and to show forth
> the utmost if love allows or demands it.
>
> *Theo-Logic I: Truth of the World,* 211

However, Balthasar also notes that truth, as self-disclosure,
would be cold were it not indwelt by goodness:

> Even the light of truth could seem cold and
> joyless if it did not also have the warmth of the

good. Indeed, a being could treat its disclosure
for itself and for others as a mere fact, without
ever feeling enriched by its own selfhood or
attracted by the prospect of knowing another.
That this is in fact *not* the case we owe to
the mutual indwelling of truth and goodness.
Because of this indwelling, in fact, the
disclosure of being is always already a
communication, while the communication
is always already an index of value.
Theo-Logic I: Truth of the World, 221–22

A crucial component of the creative power of love is the
willingness to overlook, even *forget*, aspects of the beloved
that are not congruent with the beloved's ideal self:

A further form of the veiling of truth in love [is]
the form of creative *forgetting* and overlooking[:]
... to exclude by forgetting and overlooking
whatever does not fit this image.
Theo-Logic I: Truth of the World, 215, 216

Nonetheless, there may be times when unpleasant truths
about the beloved must be brought out into the open, but
if so, this should always be done carefully and with love,
and only for the sake of love:

However unpleasant a truth may be to hear and
to say, if it is communicated and welcomed in
love, then this communication is the best thing
that could have happened.... [L]ove can seem
hard and ruthless in the administration of truth;
it can insist on pitiless unveiling, because it can

build only on the foundation of truth. Love
knows *when* this unveiling of truth is necessary
for the fruitful development of its work. For
this unveiling is not always necessary.... But
whatever is revealed (in order to be forgiven and
forgotten) may be revealed only for love's sake.
Merely knowing about something is never a
sufficient reason also for unveiling it.
Theo-Logic I: Truth of the World, 124

Love not only sets a limit to its own revelations
but also respects the mystery of the other
person. It is not in love's nature to wheedle
truth out of another's intimate space or
to extort a confession from him.
Theo-Logic I: Truth of the World, 125

People who love each other do not seek the "total self-
unveiling" of each other; rather, they want some part of
the beloved to remain a mystery, for an abiding element
of mystery is conducive to the permanence of love:

If he is himself a lover, the beloved has absolutely
no interest in the other's total self-unveiling.
What he wants instead is an object of reverence, a
permanent mystery he can go on loving forever.
Theo-Logic I: Truth of the World, 211

As Balthasar puts it, "the lover wants to know only as
much of the beloved as the beloved wants to communicate to him":

It is false to say that the intelligence naturally
strives to know everything. Prescinding from the

fact that there is infinitely much that does not
even interest the mind, the lover wants to know
only as much of the beloved as the beloved wants
to communicate to him. He would find it loveless
and shameful to spy out secrets that the beloved
had good reasons, which are always reasons of
love, for keeping silent. An urge to know that
inconsiderately tears aside every veil would very
quickly kill love. It would seek the measure of
knowing in itself outside love and thus impose
on love an alien measure. But love tolerates
no measure; it itself is the measure of all things.
The truth is the measure of being, but love is
the measure of truth.... Love, by contrast,
delights in receiving the measure of knowledge
from the hand of the beloved.
Theo-Logic I: Truth of the World, 263–64

Finally, lest the reader get the impression from some of
these passages that Balthasar thinks that loving another
person is *only* about helping the beloved grow into his true
self, i.e., to *change*, I would like to include a counterbalanc-
ing quotation, in which Balthasar expresses the importance
of appreciating the beloved for who he is right now, at this
present moment:

All love delights in letting the beloved *be*, in
every gesture and in changing moods, and
in recognizing him afresh in them.
Truth Is Symphonic, 89

Part VI

The Grand School of Love

Time is the school of exuberance, the school
of magnanimity. It is the grand school of love.
And if time is the ground of our existence,
then the ground of our existence is love. Time
is existence flowing on: love is life that pours
itself forth.... We ought to discover in the
mystery of time's duration the sweet core of
our life—the offer made by a tireless love.
Heart of the World, 25, 26

Anyone who penetrates into the mysteries
of God recognizes more and more that the
world as a whole is created "for nothing", that is,
out of a love that is free and has no other reason
behind it; that is precisely what gives it its only
plausible meaning. Recognizing or failing to
recognize this relationship will constitute the
core of the action in theo-drama.
Theo-Drama II: The Dramatis Personae: Man in God, 260

In this, the final part of this book of Balthasarian meditations on love, I would like to return to Balthasar's image of
human existence as a theo-drama, a "grand school of love"
in which our ultimate destiny hinges on our decision of
whether to open or close our hearts to love.

18

Open Heart or Closed Heart?

> The whole question is whether we accept
> God's love so that it can prove effective
> and fruitful in us, or whether we cower
> in our darkness in order to evade the light
> of this love. In the latter instance, "we hate
> the light", we hate true love, and we affirm
> our egoism in any form whatsoever.
>
> *Light of the Word*, 178

In creating us, in sustaining us in existence from moment to moment, and in giving us access to the divine life through Jesus Christ, God has opened his heart to us and invited us to join in the eternal circulation of love, sharing in the divine life of God forever. What will our response to God's invitation be? Will we open up our hearts to God and neighbor in a love that responds to God's love for us, or will we close our hearts to love and withdraw into the cramped confines of our egos? Balthasar makes it very clear that our ultimate fulfillment lies in choosing the path of opening our hearts to God in love:

> In [God] alone [the soul] can realise
> itself, though the possibility of

this realisation depends on its free
opening up of itself.
The Glory of the Lord V:
The Realm of Metaphysics in the Modern Age, 69

And yet sadly, tragically, many of us seem to choose to
close our hearts to God's invitation. We resist the invitation
because we wish to avoid the demands of self-giving love:

> The Christian faith confronts us with an
> extremely demanding image of man. It is this
> uncomfortable ideal that is the real target of
> today's intense assault on the Church's creed.
> *Explorations in Theology V: Man Is Created,* 371

> Our hearts tend to close in on themselves and
> seize on all possible excuses for avoiding the
> demand of self-transcending love. Faced with
> love's clear challenge, we become aware of
> the heart's inertia and lack of power.
> *You Crown the Year with Your Goodness,* 215

We resist God's call to *ekstasis*, the call to step out of ourselves and transcend ourselves in self-giving love, prefer-
ring the familiar confines of our egos to the infinite spaces
of the divine life:

> Man is called to pursue a supernatural goal
> and so to transcend himself.... [But man]
> always retains the urge to shut himself within
> his finitude and mortality and to content
> himself with goals at the purely natural level.
> *Theo-Drama IV: The Action,* 189–90

[Human beings speaking to God:] In [my ego] I
live, move and have my being. And I love this
ego, "for no one hates his own flesh." This space
is familiar to me.... This is my beloved dungeon:
I yearn for no freedom! By long association I have
grown fond of this prison-house of my sufferings
with all its shortcomings and all its heavy
burden.... You cannot exact the impossible feat
that I should migrate out of myself.
Heart of the World, 140, 141

This resistance to the demands of love has been referred
to for centuries as one of the seven deadly sins, the sin of
sloth or *acedia*.[1] Søren Kierkegaard (1813–1855), the Dan-
ish philosopher, referred to this resistance as the "despair
of weakness", the desire to be less than God is calling us to
be. C. S. Lewis noted that "it is natural for us to wish that
God had designed for us a less glorious and less arduous
destiny; but then we are wishing not for more love but
for less."[2] Balthasar fully agrees that the path of love is a
demanding one, but he also reiterates that this is the only
path that leads to our ultimate fulfillment as human beings:

There is ... no other path to self-fulfillment
but by dying to oneself (with Christ).
Theo-Drama IV: The Action, 190

[Jesus offers me] liberation from the
unbearable dungeon of my ego.
Heart of the World, 91

[1] Josef Pieper, *Faith, Hope, Love* (San Francisco: Ignatius Press, 1997), 192. I am
also indebted to Pieper for the subsequent references to Kierkegaard and Lewis.
[2] C. S. Lewis, *The Problem of Pain* (San Francisco: HarperSanFrancisco,
2001), 35.

> Only he who escapes from the
> prison of self is free.
>> *Convergences*, 131

Balthasar asserts that in addition to the demands of love,
there is another factor that is operative in our resistance to
God's call to love: we fear God's infinity; we fear the loss
of freedom and/or the loss of control that we think will
be associated with stepping out into the infinite spaces of
God's love; we fear "being burst asunder by God" and
therefore choose to retreat into the seeming "safety" of
our finitude:

> All creatures are finite, they have their
> measure and their limits. And when this
> finitude encounters infinite love and its
> demands, it cannot but turn of itself into a
> prison. There is in finite beings a fear of being
> burst asunder by God, and this is why they close
> themselves off when approached.
>> *Heart of the World*, 139

> If you let yourself be caught [by God's call]
> you are lost, for heavenwards there are no
> limits. He is God—accustomed to infinity.
> He sucks you upwards like a cyclone, whirls
> you up and away like a waterspout.
>> *Heart of the World*, 117

But such fear is unfounded. God seeks, not to "tear us asunder", "swallow us up", or "absorb" us, but rather to fulfill us
as unique persons who retain our personhood (and, in fact,
find our *true* personhood) within the flow of divine love:

God is so almighty that even the humblest
singular finds room in the ocean of his
divine life without having to endure (as
Hegel thought) the dissolution of its
singularity.... The living singular ... can thus
pass beyond itself, and yet as itself, in the whole
fullness of its vitality, into the encompassing
shelter of the all-life that is God himself.
Explorations in Theology V: Man Is Created, 245

Only a trinitarian God can guarantee that
man will not forfeit his independent
being when united with God.
Theo-Drama V: The Last Act, 108

[God] the Father ... draws us to him, but not
to swallow us up within him: he draws us to
him in order to fulfill us in him in a way that
transcends our own self. He is the infinite "I":
from all eternity he has wanted and chosen us
and addressed us by the familiar "thou". At this
word, "thou", uttered to each one of us in a quite
distinct and personal way, the closed doors of our
dungeon burst open.... It is this, bent upon what
is most personal and interior to us, that draws us
irresistibly beyond the closed sphere of our ego
(which makes us refer everything around us to
our own center); it draws us out of this dungeon
in which, despairing, we seem to see all beings
around us just as hopelessly imprisoned as we are.
All the religions feel their way along the prison
walls for the way out, but they miss it by taking
the seeker's great religious achievement to be the

relinquishing of his "I". In Christian terms,
what is required is not that we relinquish our
"I" but that we hand ourselves over to the
absolute "Thou" of our Origin, who
challenges us and seeks to win our love.
You Crown the Year with Your Goodness, 169–70

How far we now are from the notion that
man must negate his I or extinguish it as mere
appearance in order to enter into communication
with the infinite "I"! Rather, man now knows
himself as willed, created and affirmed in his
difference. And this consciousness does not
leave him orphaned outside God, for he
now knows that he has been willed, created
and affirmed within the divine differentiation
itself. Only in the trinitarian difference can
God be in himself the unity of love. And
when man enters into this trinitarian difference
("I no longer call you servants but friends";
"We are born of God"), he can participate in
the unity of absolute love, which now also
includes the love of one's neighbor.
Explorations in Theology IV: Spirit and Institution, 37

Thus, the *right* path, the path to human fulfillment, is the
path of openness, the path of self-giving love, the path of
Jesus Christ:

What is right and just in human terms
is the renunciation of egotism, man's openness
to the universal; in other words, love.
*The Glory of the Lord III: Studies in Theological Style:
Lay Styles*, 18

If I stay locked within myself, if I seek myself,
I shall not find the peace that is promised to
the man on whom God's favor rests. I must
go. I must enter the service of the poor and
imprisoned. I must lose my soul if I am to regain
it, for so long as I hold onto it, I shall lose it.

You Crown the Year with Your Goodness, 278

By opting to love (and hence abandoning its
closed stance), the heart allows holiness, and holy
community too, to take root within it.

You Crown the Year with Your Goodness, 214

19

Knowing Love by Doing Love

So what does Balthasar say to the person who has closed his heart to love? Give love a try! You cannot know the beauty, the goodness, or the truth of love unless you enter into and participate in the reality of love. Open yourself up to receive God's love for you and the unique mission of love God intended for you! Open yourself up to give of yourself to others and to receive the gift of self from them! Take concrete steps to enter more deeply into the reality of love: spend time with God in prayer—not just talking to God, but listening to God, meditating on God's Word and basking in God's presence and God's love for you. Read about the lives of the saints, the people who have striven so earnestly to walk the path of love. Attend Mass. Get to know some of the members of the Church who are striving to live lives of self-giving love. Give of your time and talent to people around you: family, neighbors, co-workers, etc. Volunteer time that you feel you cannot spare in order to serve others in need: at a soup kitchen, a homeless shelter, etc. Donate money to charitable causes until it hurts.

Perhaps you are not ready to take all of those steps right away, but do *something*, take even one of these steps, to begin the process of opening your heart more fully to love. Then, once you have started down the path of love, keep going deeper into love: open yourself up more fully to receive the love of God and neighbor. Give more of yourself to God and neighbor. Join the Church. Become more sacrificial. Embrace suffering out of love and offer up the fruits of your suffering for God to use for the good of others, as God sees fit. You get the idea; the key point is that you can only know the reality, the truth, of self-giving love by *doing* self-giving love:

> One does not guide someone into love in
> the same way he introduces a theoretical
> science, rather, he introduces someone to
> love by permitting him to participate in love's
> reality, by teaching him to love within the
> all-encompassing love of God.
> *Light of the Word,* 199

> Absolute fullness ... does not consist of
> "having", but of "being=giving". It is in giving
> that one is and has. This cannot be explained
> in words ... it can only be done, and be
> understood in the course of doing it.
> *The Glory of the Lord VII: Theology:*
> *The New Covenant,* 391

> The love which "surpasses knowledge" can only
> be "known" (Eph 3:19) in something more-than-
> knowledge, which is in fact love itself, a loving
> together with God and from God.
> *Prayer,* 217–18

> He who "does" the word will understand it;
> and those who do it frequently will gain
> a greater understanding of it than others.

Every lover is a knower; he "knows God
... for God is love", whereas the one
who does not love is in ignorance.

Prayer, 215

The *good* which God does to us can only be
experienced as the *truth* if we share in *performing* it
(Jn 7:17; 8:31f.); we must "do the truth in love"
(*aletheuein en agape* [Eph 4:15]) not only in order
to perceive the truth of the good but, equally, in
order to embody it increasingly in the world.

Theo-Drama I: Prolegomena, 20

"Walking in the truth" is the way the believer
possesses the truth (2 Jn 1–4; 3 Jn 3–4, etc.).

Explorations in Theology I: The Word Made Flesh, 181–82

This is the true sense of the existential character of
truth; we only really possess it, when we do it; it
has not only to be grasped and seen in concepts,
but expressed in the whole of one's being and life.

Explorations in Theology I: The Word Made Flesh, 233

[Philosophers] will tell [the novice], and rightly
so, that the man who does not dare to jump
into the water will never learn what it means to
swim and that the man who does not dare
to jump into the truth will never attain the
certainty that truth in fact exists.

Theo-Logic I: Truth of the World, 25

The rightness of the form of revelation, initially
"seen" in faith—the form to which the believer
surrenders and entrusts himself—is *confirmed*
within this existence of self-surrender as being

true and correct, and this gives the believer
a new form of Christian certitude which
can be called "Christian experience".
The Glory of the Lord I: Seeing the Form, 219

This experience can be acquired in no
way other than by having it, and only he
can have it who surrenders himself to
the movement of the journey.
The Glory of the Lord I: Seeing the Form, 222

Our life is a gift and a giving to others;
therefore, it is joy at a profound level. Anyone
who seriously makes this idea his own and
begins to practice it will find it to be true; he
will discover that the will to live it out, that is,
to accept everything as a gift from God, can
transform our life right down to its roots.
You Crown the Year with Your Goodness, 29

20

The Perfect Feat of Daring

I would like to close this book of Balthasarian meditations on love with two final quotations, both of which focus on Jesus Christ's invitation to each of us to join in the eternal circulation of love, to take the leap out of the finitude of our self-enclosed egos and into the infinite flow of self-giving love that is the divine life:

> Soft it approaches, almost inaudible and
> yet quite unavoidable: a ray of light, an
> offer of power, a command that is more and
> less than a command—a wish, a request, an
> invitation, an enticement: brief as an instant,
> simple to grasp as the glance of two eyes.
> It contains a promise: love, delight and a
> vision extending over an immense and
> vertiginous distance. Liberation from the
> unbearable dungeon of my ego. The adventure
> I had always longed for. The perfect feat of
> daring in which I am sure to win all only
> by losing all. The source of life opening up
> inexhaustibly to me, who am dying of thirst!
> *Heart of the World*, 91–92

Dare to make the leap into the Light!... What
could be simpler and sweeter than opening the
door to love? What could be easier than falling to
one's knees and saying: "My Lord and my God!"?
Heart of the World, 165

BIBLIOGRAPHY

Works by Hans Urs von Balthasar (sole author)

The Christian and Anxiety. Translated by Dennis D. Martin and Michael J. Miller. San Francisco: Ignatius Press, 2000.

Christian Meditation. Translated by Sister Mary Theresilde Skerry. San Francisco: Ignatius Press, 1989.

The Christian State of Life. Translated by Sister Mary Frances McCarthy. San Francisco: Ignatius Press, 1983.

Convergences: To the Source of Christian Mystery. Translated by E. A. Nelson. San Francisco: Ignatius Press, 1983.

Credo: Meditations on the Apostles' Creed. Translated by David Kipp. San Francisco: Ignatius Press, 1990.

Dare We Hope "That All Men Be Saved"? Translated by Dr. David Kipp and Rev. Lothar Krauth. 2nd ed., 1988; San Francisco: Ignatius Press, 2014.

Elucidations. Translated by John Riches. San Francisco: Ignatius Press, 1998.

Engagement with God. Translated by R. John Halliburton. San Francisco: Ignatius Press, 2008.

Epilogue. Translated by Edward T. Oakes. San Francisco: Ignatius Press, 2004.

Explorations in Theology. Vol. 1, *The Word Made Flesh*, translated by A. V. Littledale with Alexander Dru. San Francisco: Ignatius Press, 1989.

Explorations in Theology. Vol. 2, *Spouse of the Word*, translated by A. V. Littledale with Alexander Dru. San Francisco: Ignatius Press, 1991.

Explorations in Theology. Vol. 3, *Creator Spirit*, translated by Brian McNeil, C.R.V. San Francisco: Ignatius Press, 1993.

Explorations in Theology. Vol. 4, *Spirit and Institution*, translated by Edward T. Oakes. San Francisco: Ignatius Press, 1995.

Explorations in Theology. Vol. 5, *Man Is Created*, translated by Adrian Walker. San Francisco: Ignatius Press, 2014.

"The Fathers, the Scholastics, and Ourselves." *Communio: International Catholic Review* XXIV (2) (1997): 347–96.

The Glory of the Lord: A Theological Aesthetics. Vol. 1, *Seeing the Form*, translated by Erasmo Leiva-Merikakis. San Francisco: Ignatius Press, 2009.

The Glory of the Lord: A Theological Aesthetics. Vol. 2, *Studies in Theological Style: Clerical Styles*, edited by John Riches; translated by Andrew Louth, Francis McDonagh, and Brian McNeil, C.R.V. San Francisco: Ignatius Press, 1984.

The Glory of the Lord: A Theological Aesthetics. Vol. 3, *Studies in Theological Style: Lay Styles*, edited by John Riches; translated by Andrew Louth, John Saward, Martin Simon, and Rowan Williams. San Francisco: Ignatius Press, 1986.

The Glory of the Lord: A Theological Aesthetics. Vol. 4, *The Realm of Metaphysics in Antiquity*, edited by John Riches; translated by Brian McNeil, C.R.V., Andrew Louth, John Saward, Rowan Williams, and Oliver Davies. San Francisco: Ignatius Press, 1989.

The Glory of the Lord: A Theological Aesthetics. Vol. 5, *The Realm of Metaphysics in the Modern Age*, edited by Brian McNeil, C.R.V., and John Riches; translated by Oliver Davies, Andrew Louth, Brian McNeil, C.R.V., John Saward, and Rowan Williams. San Francisco: Ignatius Press, 1991.

The Glory of the Lord: A Theological Aesthetics. Vol. 6, *Theology: The Old Covenant*, edited by John Riches; translated by Brian McNeil, C.R.V., and Erasmo Leiva-Merikakis. San Francisco: Ignatius Press, 1991.

The Glory of the Lord: A Theological Aesthetics. Vol. 7, *Theology: The New Covenant*, edited by John Riches; translated by Brian McNeil, C.R.V. San Francisco: Ignatius Press, 1989.

The Grain of Wheat: Aphorisms. Translated by Erasmo Leiva-Merikakis. San Francisco: Ignatius Press, 1995.

Heart of the World. Translated by Erasmo S. Leiva. San Francisco: Ignatius Press, 1979.

In the Fullness of Faith: On the Centrality of the Distinctively Catholic. Translated by Graham Harrison. San Francisco: Ignatius Press, 1988.

Life Out of Death: Meditations on the Paschal Mystery. Translated by Martina Stöckl. San Francisco: Ignatius Press, 2012.

Light of the Word: Brief Reflections on the Sunday Readings. Translated by Dennis D. Martin. San Francisco: Ignatius Press, 1983.

Love Alone Is Credible. Translated by D. C. Schindler. San Francisco: Ignatius Press, 2004.

Mary for Today. Translated by Robert Nowell. San Francisco: Ignatius Press, 1988.

The Moment of Christian Witness. Translated by Richard Beckley. San Francisco: Ignatius Press, 1994.

Mysterium Paschale: The Mystery of Easter. Translated by Aidan Nichols, O.P. San Francisco: Ignatius Press, 2005.

My Work: In Retrospect. San Francisco: Ignatius Press, 1993.

New Elucidations. Translated by Sister Mary Theresilde Skerry. San Francisco: Ignatius Press, 1986.

Prayer. Translated by Graham Harrison. San Francisco: Ignatius Press, 1986.

A Short Primer for Unsettled Laymen. Translated by Michael Waldstein, 1985; San Francisco: Ignatius Press, 2020.

Test Everything: Hold Fast to What Is Good. Translated by Maria Shrady. San Francisco: Ignatius Press, 1989.

A Theological Anthropology. New York: Sheed and Ward, 1968.

Theo-Drama: Theological Dramatic Theory. Vol. 1, *Prolegomena*, translated by Graham Harrison. San Francisco: Ignatius Press, 1988.

Theo-Drama: Theological Dramatic Theory. Vol. 2, *The Dramatis Personae: Man in God*, translated by Graham Harrison. San Francisco: Ignatius Press, 1990.

Theo-Drama: Theological Dramatic Theory. Vol. 3, *The Dramatis Personae: The Person in Christ*, translated by Graham Harrison. San Francisco: Ignatius Press, 1992.

Theo-Drama: Theological Dramatic Theory. Vol. 4, *The Action*, translated by Graham Harrison. San Francisco: Ignatius Press, 1994.

Theo-Drama: Theological Dramatic Theory. Vol. 5, *The Last Act*, translated by Graham Harrison. San Francisco: Ignatius Press, 1998.

Theo-Logic: Theological Logical Theory. Vol. 1, *Truth of the World*, translated by Adrian J. Walker. San Francisco: Ignatius Press, 2000.

Theo-Logic: Theological Logical Theory. Vol. 2, *Truth of God*, translated by Adrian J. Walker. San Francisco: Ignatius Press, 2004.

Theo-Logic: Theological Logical Theory. Vol. 3, *The Spirit of Truth*, translated by Graham Harrison. San Francisco: Ignatius Press, 2005.

A Theology of History. San Francisco: Ignatius Press, 1994.

The Threefold Garland: The World's Salvation in Mary's Prayer. Translated by Erasmo Leiva-Merikakis. San Francisco: Ignatius Press, 1985.

Truth Is Symphonic: Aspects of Christian Pluralism. Translated by Graham Harrison. San Francisco: Ignatius Press, 1987.

Two Sisters in the Spirit: Thérèse of Lisieux & Elizabeth of the Trinity. Translated by Donald Nichols, Anne Englund Nash, and Dennis Martin. San Francisco: Ignatius Press, 1992.

Unless You Become Like This Child. Translated by Erasmo Leiva-Merikakis. San Francisco: Ignatius Press, 1991.

Who Is a Christian? Translated by Frank Davidson. San Francisco: Ignatius Press, 2014.

You Crown the Year with Your Goodness. Translated by Graham Harrison. San Francisco: Ignatius Press, 1989.

You Have Words of Eternal Life: Scripture Meditations. Translated by Dennis Martin. San Francisco: Ignatius Press, 1991.

Works Coauthored by Hans Urs von Balthasar

Balthasar, Hans Urs von, and Adrienne von Speyr. *To the Heart of the Mystery of Redemption.* Translated by Anne Englund Nash. San Francisco: Ignatius Press, 2010.

Ratzinger, Joseph Cardinal, and Balthasar, Hans Urs von. *Mary: The Church at the Source.* Translated by Adrian Walker. San Francisco: Ignatius Press, 2005.

Works by Authors Other than Hans Urs von Balthasar

Barrett, Melanie Susan. *Love's Beauty at the Heart of the Christian Moral Life: The Ethics of Catholic Theologian Hans Urs von Balthasar.* Lewiston, Australia: Edwin Mellen Press, 2009.

Bartlett, John. *Bartlett's Familiar Quotations.* Seventeenth edition, edited by Justin Kaplan. Boston: Little, Brown, 2002.

Benedict XVI. *God Is Love: Deus Caritas Est.* San Francisco: Ignatius Press, 2006.

Dalzell, Thomas G. *The Dramatic Encounter of Divine and Human Freedom in the Theology of Hans Urs von Balthasar.* New York: Peter Lang, 2000.

De Lubac, Henri Cardinal, S.J. "A Witness of Christ in the Church: Hans Urs von Balthasar." In *Hans Urs von Balthasar: His Life and Work,* edited by David L. Schindler, 271–88. San Francisco: Ignatius Press, 1991.

Gawronski, Raymond, S.J. *Word and Silence: Hans Urs von Balthasar and the Spiritual Encounter between East and West.* Grand Rapids, Mich.: Eerdmans, 1995.

Healy, Nicholas J. *The Eschatology of Hans Urs von Balthasar: Being as Communion.* Oxford: Oxford University Press, 2005.

Henrici, Peter, S.J. "Hans Urs von Balthasar: A Sketch of His Life." In *Hans Urs von Balthasar: His Life and Work,* edited by David L. Schindler, 7–43. San Francisco: Ignatius Press, 1991.

———. "The Philosophy of Hans Urs von Balthasar." In *Hans Urs von Balthasar: His Life and Work,* edited by David L. Schindler, 149–67. San Francisco: Ignatius Press, 1991.

Howsare, Rodney A. *Balthasar: A Guide for the Perplexed.* New York: T&T Clark, 2009.

The Ignatius Catholic Study Bible: The New Testament. Revised Standard Version, Second Catholic Edition. San Francisco: Ignatius Press, 2010.

John Paul II. "Telegram from Pope John Paul II." In *Hans Urs von Balthasar: His Life and Work*, edited by David L. Schindler, 289. San Francisco: Ignatius Press, 1991.

Kay, Jeffrey Ames. *Theological Aesthetics: The Role of Aesthetics in the Theological Method of Hans Urs von Balthasar*. Bern: Herbert Lang, 1975.

Lehman, Karl, and Walter Kasper. "Preface to *Hans Urs von Balthasar: Gestalt und Werk*." In *Hans Urs von Balthasar: His Life and Work*, edited by David L. Schindler, 267–69. San Francisco: Ignatius Press, 1991.

Lewis, C. S. *The Four Loves*. San Francisco: HarperOne, 2017.

———. *The Problem of Pain*. San Francisco: HarperOne, 2017.

McIntosh, Mark A. *Christology from Within: Spirituality and the Incarnation in Hans Urs von Balthasar*. Notre Dame, Ind.: University of Notre Dame Press, 2000.

Murphy, Francesca Aran. *Christ the Form of Beauty: A Study in Theology and Literature*. Edinburgh: T&T Clark, 1995.

Nichols, Aidan, O.P. *Divine Fruitfulness: A Guide through Balthasar's Theology beyond the Trilogy*. Washington, D.C.: Catholic University of America Press, 2007.

———. *A Key to Balthasar: Hans Urs von Balthasar on Beauty, Goodness, and Truth*. Grand Rapids, Mich.: Baker Academic, 2011.

———. *No Bloodless Myth: A Guide through Balthasar's Dramatics*. Washington, D.C.: Catholic University of America Press, 2000.

———. *Say It Is Pentecost: A Guide through Balthasar's Logic*. Washington, D.C.: Catholic University of America Press, 2001.

———. *Scattering the Seed: A Guide through Balthasar's Early Writings on Philosophy and the Arts*. Washington, D.C.: Catholic University of America Press, 2006.

———. *The Word Has Been Abroad: A Guide through Balthasar's Aesthetics*. Washington, D.C.: Catholic University of America Press, 1998.

Oakes, Edward T. *Pattern of Redemption*. New York: Continuum, 1997.

Ouellet, Marc Cardinal. *Divine Likeness: Toward a Trinitarian Anthropology of the Family.* Grand Rapids, Mich.: Eerdmans, 2006.

Pieper, Josef. *Faith, Hope, Love.* San Francisco: Ignatius Press, 1997.

Rahner, Karl. "Hans Urs von Balthasar." In *Civitas* 1965, p. 604, cited in Jeffery Ames Kay, *Theological Aesthetics: The Role of Aesthetics in the Theological Method of Hans Urs von Balthasar,* p. viii. Bern: Herbert Lang, 1975.

Ratzinger, Joseph Cardinal. "Homily at the Funeral Liturgy of Hans Urs von Balthasar." In *Hans Urs von Balthasar: His Life and Work,* edited by David L. Schindler, 291–95. San Francisco: Ignatius Press, 1991.

Schindler, David L., ed. *Hans Urs von Balthasar: His Life and Work.* San Francisco: Ignatius Press, 1991.

Scola, Angelo. *Hans Urs von Balthasar: A Theological Style.* Grand Rapids, Mich.: Eerdmans, 1995.

Speyr, Adrienne von. "The Fire of God Is a Suffering." In *To the Heart of the Mystery of Redemption,* edited by Hans Urs von Balthasar and Adrienne von Speyr, 73–74. San Francisco: Ignatius Press, 2010.